# Berlitz®

The everyday world at your fingertips

# German
## picture dictionary

www.berlitzpublishing.com

BERLIN

**Distribution**

UK, Ireland and Europe:
Apa Publications (UK) Ltd;
sales@insightguides.com
United States and Canada:
Ingram Publisher Services;
ips@ingramcontent.com
Australia and New Zealand:
Woodslane; info@woodslane.com.au
Southeast Asia:
Apa Publications (SN) Pte;
singaporeoffice@insightguides.com
Worldwide: Apa Publications (UK) Ltd;
sales@insightguides.com

**Special Sales, Content Licensing
and CoPublishing**

Insight Guides can be purchased in bulk
quantities at discounted prices. We can
create special editions, personalised
jackets and corporate imprints tailored to
your needs. sales@insightguides.com;
www.insightguides.biz

First Edition 2017

Printed in China by CTPS

**Contact us**

Every effort has been made to provide
accurate information in this publication,
but changes are inevitable. The publisher
cannot be responsible for any resulting
loss, inconvenience or injury. We would
appreciate it if readers would call our
attention to any errors or outdated
information. We also welcome your
suggestions; please contact us at:
berlitz@apaguide.co.uk

**Series Editor:** Carine Tracanelli
**Editor:** Urszula Krajewska
**Head of Production:** Rebeka Davies
**Series design:** Krzysztof Kop
**Picture research & DTP design:**
Tamkapress
**English text:** Carine Tracanelli &
Barbara Marchwica
**Translation & simplified phonetics:**
ILS AT
**Photo credits:** all Shutterstock and Fotolia

# Introduction

Whether you are a total beginner or already have a sound knowledge of your chosen language, this Berlitz picture dictionary will help you to communicate quickly and easily. Packed with 2,000 useful terms, it covers all everyday situations, whether you're applying for a job, going shopping or just getting around. See, understand, memorise: visual learning by combining a word with an image helps you remember it more effectively as images affect us more than text alone.

To get the most out of your picture dictionary you can search for words in two ways: by theme (women's clothes, sporting facilities, hobbies, etc.) or by consulting the index at the end. You'll also find important phrases surrounding a topic in each chapter, ensuring that you have the foundations you need for communicating.

Each word is followed by its phonetic transcription to make sure you pronounce each word or sentence correctly. You will find a helpful guide to pronunciation in your chosen language on pages 7–10.

Note that the terms in this picture dictionary are always given in their singular form unless they are generally only used in their plural form, and all nouns are preceded by their gender-specific article. Certain terms are not gender-neutral and in such cases all genders are provided throughout in both the translation and phonetic transcription, ensuring you can communicate in all variants.

Berlitz are renowned for the quality and expertise of their language products. Discover the full range at www.berlitzpublishing.com.

# Table of Contents

# Pronunciation

This section is designed to make you familiar with the sounds of German, using our simplified phonetic transcription. You'll find the pronunciation of the German letters explained below, together with their "imitated" equivalents. This system is used throughout the picture dictionary; simply read the pronunciation as if it were English, noting any special rules below.

The German alphabet is the same as English, with the addition of the letter **ß**. Some vowels appear with an Umlaut: **ä**, **ü** and **ö**. Of note, German recently underwent a spelling reform. The letter **ß** is now shown as **ss** after a short vowel, but is unchanged after a long vowel or diphthong. In print and dated material, you may still see the **ß**; e.g. formerly *Kuß*, now *Kuss*.

Stress has been indicated in the phonetic transcription: the capital letters should be pronounced with more stress than others, e.g. Adresse: ah-DREH-suh.

**Consonants**

| Letter(s) | Approximate Pronunciation | Symbol | Example | Pronunciation |
|---|---|---|---|---|
| b | 1. at the end of a word or between a vowel and a consonant, like p in *up* | p | **ab** | ahp |
| | 2. elsewhere, as in English | b | **bis** | bihs |
| c | 1. before e, i, ä and ö, like ts in *hits* | ts | **Celsius** | TSEHL-see-oos |
| | 2. elsewhere, like c in *cat* | k | **Café** | kah-FEH |
| ch | 1. like k in *kit* | k | **Wachs** | vahks |
| | 2. after vowels, like ch in *Scottish loch* | kh | **doch** | dohkh |
| | 3. like s in *sure* | sh | **speichern** | SHPIE-shern |
| d | 1. at the end of the word or before a consonant, like t in *eat* | t | **Rad** | raht |
| | 2. elsewhere, like d in *do* | d | **danke** | DAHN-kuh |
| g | 1. at the end of a word, sounds like k | k | **fertig** | FEHR-tihk |
| | 2. like g in *go* | g | **gehen** | GEH-yehn |
| | 3. in foreign words, like g in *age* | g | **Teenager** | TEE-neh-gehr |
| j | like y in *yes* | y | **ja** | yah |
| qu | like k + v | kv | **Quark** | kvahrk |
| r | pronounced in the back of the mouth | r | **warum** | vah-ROOM |
| s | 1. before or between vowels, like z in *zoo* | z | **sie** | zee |
| | 2. before p and t, like sh in *shut* | sh | **Sport** | shpohrt |
| | 3. elsewhere, like s in *sit* | s | **es ist** | ehs ihst |
| ß | like s in *sit* | s | **groß** | grohs |

| sch | like sh in *shut* | sh | **schnell** | shnehl |
|-----|-------------------|-----|-------------|--------|
| tsch | like ch in *chip* | ch | **deutsch** | doych |
| tz | like ts in *hits* | ts | **Platz** | plahts |
| v | 1. like f in *for* | f | **vier** | feer |
| | 2. in foreign words, like v in *voice* | v | **Vase** | VAH-zuh |
| w | like v in *voice* | v | **wie** | vee |
| z | like ts in *hits* | ts | **zeigen** | TSIE-gehn |
| dsch | like j in *jet* | dch | **Fidschi** | FEE-dchih |

Letters f, h, k, l, m, n, p, t and x are pronounced as in English.

**Vowels**

| Letter(s) | Approximate Pronunciation | Symbol | Example | Pronunciation |
|-----------|---------------------------|--------|---------|---------------|
| a | like a in *father* | ah | **Tag** | tahk |
| ä | 1. like e in *let* | eh | **Lärm** | lehrm |
| e | 1. like e in *let* | eh | **schnell** | shnehl |
| | 3. at the end of a word, if the syllable is not stressed, like u in *us* | uh | **bitte** | BIH-tuh |
| i | 1. like i in *hit*, before a consonant or doubled consonant | ih | **billig** | BIH-lihk |
| | 2. otherwise, like ee in *meet* | ee | **ihm** | eem |
| o | like o in *fog* | oh | **voll** | fohl |
| ö | like er in *fern* | er | **schön** | shern |

| | | | | |
|---|---|---|---|---|
| u | like oo in *boot* | oo | **Nuss** | noos |
| ü | like ew in *new* | ew | **über** | EW-behr |
| y | like ew in *new* | ew | **typisch** | TEW-pihsh |

## Combined Vowels

| Letter(s) | Approximate Pronunciation | Symbol | Example | Pronunciation |
|---|---|---|---|---|
| ai, ay, ei, ey | like ie in *tie* | ie | **nein** | nien |
| au | like ow in *now* | ow | **auf** | owf |
| äu, eu | like oy in *boy* | oy | **neu** | noy |
| ie | like ee in *meet* | ee | **sie** | zee |

# GENERAL VOCABULARY

first name
**der Vorname**
dehr FOHR-nah-muh

date of birth
**das Geburtsdatum**
dahs geh-BOORTS-dah-toom

place of birth
**der Geburtsort**
dehr geh-BOORTS-ohrt

email address
**die E-Mail-Adresse**
dee EE-mehyl-ah-DREH-suh

phone number
**die Telefonnummer**
dee teh-leh-FOHN-noo-mehr

last name
**der Familienname**
dehr fah-MEE-leeuhn-nah-muh

age
**das Alter**
dahs AHL-tehr

| | | |
|---|---|---|
| address | **die Adresse** | dee ah-DREH-suh |
| marital status | **der Familienstand** | dehr fah-MEE-leeuhn-shtahnt |
| children | **die Kinder** | dee KIHN-dehr |
| home country | **das Heimatland** | dahs HIE-maht-lahnt |
| place of residence | **der Wohnort** | dehr VOHN-ohrt |
| single | **ledig** | LEH-dihk |
| in a relationship | **in einer Beziehung** | ihn IE-nehr beh-TSEE-yoonk |
| divorced | **geschieden** | geh-SHEE-dehn |
| married | **verheiratet** | fehr-HIE-rah-teht |
| widowed | **verwitwet** | fehr-VIHT-veht |
| What's your name? | **Wie heißt du / heißen Sie?** | vee hiest doo / HIE-sehn zee? |
| Where are you from? | **Woher kommst du / kommen Sie?** | voh-HEHR kohmst doo / KOH-mehn zee? |
| Where were you born? | **Wo bist du / sind Sie geboren?** | voh bihst doo / zihnt zee geh-BOH-rehn? |
| When were you born? | **Wann bist du / sind Sie geboren?** | vahn bihst doo / zihnt zee geh-BOH-rehn? |
| What is your address? | **Wie ist deine / Ihre Adresse?** | vee ihst DIE-nuh / EE-ruh ah-DREH-suh? |
| What's your phone number? | **Wie ist deine / Ihre Telefonnummer?** | vee ihst DIE-nuh / EE-ruh teh-leh-FOHN-noo-mehr? |
| Are you married? | **Bist du / Sind Sie verheiratet?** | bihst doo / zihnt zee vehr-HIE-rah-teht? |
| Do you have children? | **Hast du / Haben Sie Kinder?** | hahst doo / HAH-behn zee KIHN-dehr? |

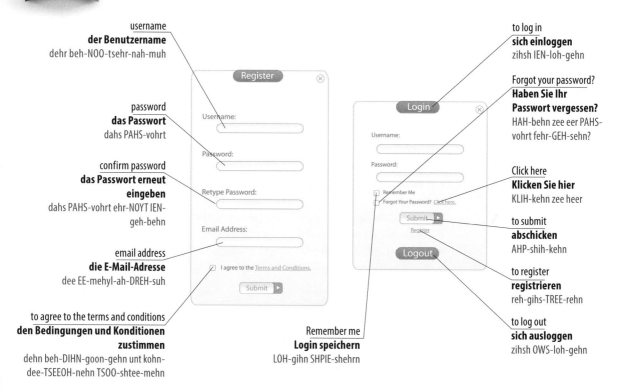

username
**der Benutzername**
dehr beh-NOO-tsehr-nah-muh

password
**das Passwort**
dahs PAHS-vohrt

confirm password
**das Passwort erneut eingeben**
dahs PAHS-vohrt ehr-NOYT IEN-geh-behn

email address
**die E-Mail-Adresse**
dee EE-mehyl-ah-DREH-suh

to agree to the terms and conditions
**den Bedingungen und Konditionen zustimmen**
dehn beh-DIHN-goon-gehn unt kohn-dee-TSEEOH-nehn TSOO-shtee-mehn

to log in
**sich einloggen**
zihsh IEN-loh-gehn

Forgot your password?
**Haben Sie Ihr Passwort vergessen?**
HAH-behn zee eer PAHS-vohrt fehr-GEH-sehn?

Click here
**Klicken Sie hier**
KLIH-kehn zee heer

to submit
**abschicken**
AHP-shih-kehn

to register
**registrieren**
reh-gihs-TREE-rehn

to log out
**sich ausloggen**
zihsh OWS-loh-gehn

Remember me
**Login speichern**
LOH-gihn SHPIE-shehrn

| 0 | zero | **null** | nool |
|---|---|---|---|
| 1 | one | **eins** | iens |
| 2 | two | **zwei** | tsvie |
| 3 | three | **drei** | drie |
| 4 | four | **vier** | feer |
| 5 | five | **fünf** | fewnf |
| 6 | six | **sechs** | zehks |
| 7 | seven | **sieben** | ZEE-behn |
| 8 | eight | **acht** | ahkht |
| 9 | nine | **neun** | noyn |
| 10 | ten | **zehn** | tsehn |
| 11 | eleven | **elf** | ehlf |
| 12 | twelve | **zwölf** | tsverlf |
| 13 | thirteen | **dreizehn** | DRIE-tsehn |
| 14 | fourteen | **vierzehn** | FEER-tsehn |
| 15 | fifteen | **fünfzehn** | FEWNF-tsehn |
| 16 | sixteen | **sechzehn** | ZEHSH-tsehn |

| 17 | seventeen | **siebzehn** | ZEEP-tsehn |
|---|---|---|---|
| 18 | eighteen | **achtzehn** | AHKHT-tsehn |
| 19 | nineteen | **neunzehn** | NOYN-tsehn |
| 20 | twenty | **zwanzig** | TSVAHN-tsihk |
| 21 | twenty-one | **einundzwanzig** | IEN-oont-tsvahn-tsihk |
| 30 | thirty | **dreißig** | DRIE-sihk |
| 40 | forty | **vierzig** | FEER-tsihk |
| 50 | fifty | **fünfzig** | FEWNF-tsihk |
| 60 | sixty | **sechzig** | ZEHKH-tsihk |
| 70 | seventy | **siebzig** | ZEEP-tsihk |
| 80 | eighty | **achtzig** | AHKHT-tsihk |
| 90 | ninety | **neunzig** | NOYN-tsihk |
| 100 | one hundred | **einhundert** | ien-HOON-dehrt |
| 101 | one hundred and one | **einhundertundeins** | ien-HOON-dehrt-oont-iens |
| 1000 | one thousand | **eintausend** | ein-TOW-zehnt |
| 1 000 000 | one million | **eine Million** | IE-nuh mee-lee-OHN |

1st (first)
**der/die/das erste**
dehr/dee/dahs EHRS-tuh

2nd (second)
**der/die/das zweite**
dehr/dee/dahs TSVIE-tuh

3rd (third)
**der/die/das dritte**
dehr/dee/dahs DRIH-tuh

| | | **der/die/das** | dehr/dee/dahs |
|---|---|---|---|
| | | **...** | ... |
| 4th | fourth | **vierte** | FEER-tuh |
| 5th | fifth | **fünfte** | FEWNF-tuh |
| 6th | sixth | **sechste** | ZEHKS-tuh |
| 7th | seventh | **siebte** | ZEEP-tuh |
| 8th | eighth | **achte** | AHKH-tuh |
| 9th | ninth | **neunte** | NOYN-tuh |
| 10th | tenth | **zehnte** | TSEHN-tuh |
| 11th | eleventh | **elfte** | EHLF-tuh |
| 12th | twelfth | **zwölfte** | TSVERLF-tuh |

| 13th | thirteenth | **dreizehnte** | DRIE-tsehn-tuh |
|---|---|---|---|
| 14th | fourteenth | **vierzehnte** | FEER-tsehn-tuh |
| 15th | fifteenth | **fünfzehnte** | FEWNF-tsehn-tuh |
| 16th | sixteenth | **sechzehnte** | ZEHSH-tsehn-tuh |
| 17th | seventeenth | **siebzehnte** | ZEEP-tsehn-tuh |
| 18th | eighteenth | **achtzehnte** | AHKHT-tsehn-tuh |
| 19th | nineteenth | **neunzehnte** | NOYN-tsehn-tuh |
| 20th | twentieth | **zwanzigste** | TSVAHN-tsihsh-stuh |
| 21st | twenty-first | **einundzwanzigste** | IEN-oont-TSVAHN-tsihsh-stuh |
| 22nd | twenty-second | **zweiundzwanzigste** | TSVIE-oont-TSVAHN-tsihsh-stuh |
| 23rd | twenty-third | **dreiundzwanzigste** | DRIE-oont-TSVAHN-tsihsh-stuh |
| 24th | twenty-fourth | **vierundzwanzigste** | FEER-oont-TSVAHN-tsihsh-stuh |
| 25th | twenty-fifth | **fünfundzwanzigste** | FEWNF-oont-TSVAHN-tsihsh-stuh |
| 26th | twenty-sixth | **sechsundzwanzigste** | ZEHKS-oont-TSVAHN-tsihsh-stuh |
| 27th | twenty-seventh | **siebenundzwanzigste** | ZEE-behn-oont-TSVAHN-tsihsh-stuh |
| 28th | twenty-eighth | **achtundzwanzigste** | AHKHT-oont-TSVAHN-tsihsh-stuh |
| 29th | twenty-ninth | **neunundzwanzigste** | NOYN-oont-TSVAHN-tsihsh-stuh |
| 30th | thirtieth | **dreißigste** | DRIE-sihsh-stuh |
| 40th | fortieth | **vierzigste** | FEER-tsihsh-stuh |
| 50th | fiftieth | **fünfzigste** | FEWNF-tsihsh-stuh |
| 60th | sixtieth | **sechzigste** | SEHSH-tsihsh-stuh |
| 70th | seventieth | **siebzigste** | ZEEP-tsihsh-stuh |
| 80th | eightieth | **achtzigste** | AHKHT-tsihsh-stuh |
| 90th | ninetieth | **neunzigste** | NOYN-tsihsh-stuh |
| 100th | hundredth | **hundertste** | HOON-dehrt-stuh |

| noon | **der Mittag** | dehr MIH-tahk |
|---|---|---|
| midnight | **die Mitternacht** | dee MIH-tehr-nahkht |

| one am | **ein Uhr** | ien oor |
|---|---|---|
| one pm | **dreizehn Uhr** | DRIE-tsehn oor |

| two am | **zwei Uhr** | tsvie oor |
|---|---|---|
| two pm | **vierzehn Uhr** | FEER-tsehn oor |

| three am | **drei Uhr** | drie oor |
|---|---|---|
| three pm | **fünfzehn Uhr** | FEWNF-tsehn oor |

| four am | **vier Uhr** | feer oor |
|---|---|---|
| four pm | **sechzehn Uhr** | ZEHSH-tsehn oor |

| five am | **fünf Uhr** | fewnf oor |
|---|---|---|
| five pm | **siebzehn Uhr** | ZEEP-tsehn oor |

| six am | **sechs Uhr** | zehks oor |
|---|---|---|
| six pm | **achtzehn Uhr** | AHKHT-tsehn oor |

| seven am | **sieben Uhr** | ZEE-behn oor |
|---|---|---|
| seven pm | **neunzehn Uhr** | NOYN-tsehn oor |

| eight am | **acht Uhr** | ahkht oor |
|---|---|---|
| eight pm | **zwanzig Uhr** | TSVAHN-tsihk oor |

| nine am | **neun Uhr** | noyn oor |
|---|---|---|
| nine pm | **einundzwanzig Uhr** | IEN-oont-tsvahn-tsihk oor |

| ten am | **zehn Uhr** | tsehn oor |
|---|---|---|
| ten pm | **zweiundzwanzig Uhr** | TSVIE-oont-tsvahn-tsihk oor |

| eleven am | **elf Uhr** | ehlf oor |
|---|---|---|
| eleven pm | **dreiundzwanzig Uhr** | DRIE-oont-tsvahn-tsihk oor |

quarter to
**Viertel vor**
FEER-tehl fohr

ten to
**zehn vor**
tsehn fohr

five to
**fünf vor**
fewnf fohr

... o'clock
**... Uhr**
... oor

five past
**fünf nach**
fewnf nahkh

ten past
**zehn nach**
tsehn nahkh

quarter past
**Viertel nach**
FEER-tehl nahkh

half past
**halb**
hahlp

| What time is it? | **Wie spät ist es?** | vee shpeht ihst ehs? |
|---|---|---|
| It's nine thirty. | **Es ist neun Uhr dreißig.** | ehs ihst NOYN oor DRIE-sihk |
| Excuse me, could you tell me the time please? | **Entschuldigen Sie. Könnten Sie mir bitte sagen, wie spät es ist?** | ehnt-SHOOL-dee-gehn zee. KERN-tehn zee meer bih-tuh ZAH-gehn, vee shpeht ehs ihst? |
| It's about half past nine. | **Es ist ungefähr halb zehn.** | ehs ihst OON-geh-fehr hahlp tsehn |

Monday
**der Montag**
dehr MOHN-tahk

Tuesday
**der Dienstag**
dehr DEENS-tahk

Wednesday
**der Mittwoch**
dehr MEET-vohkh

Thursday
**der Donnerstag**
dehr DOH-nehrs-tahk

Friday
**der Freitag**
dehr FRIE-tahk

Saturday
**der Samstag**
dehr ZAHMS-tahk

Sunday
**der Sonntag**
dehr ZOHN-tahk

| on Monday | **am Montag** | ahm MOHN-tahk |
| from Tuesday | **seit Dienstag** | ziet DEENS-tahk |
| until Wednesday | **bis Mittwoch** | bihs MIHT-vohkh |

### JANUARY

January
**der Januar**
dehr YAH-noo-ahr

### FEBRUARY

February
**der Februar**
dehr FEH-broo-ahr

### MARCH

March
**der März**
dehr mehrts

### APRIL

April
**der April**
dehr ah-PRIHL

### MAY

May
**der Mai**
dehr mi

### JUNE

June
**der Juni**
dehr YOO-nee

### JULY

July
**der Juli**
dehr YOO-lee

### AUGUST

August
**der August**
dehr ow-GOOST

### SEPTEMBER

September
**der September**
dehr zehp-TEHM-behr

### OCTOBER

October
**der Oktober**
dehr ohk-TOH-behr

### NOVEMBER

November
**der November**
dehr noh-VEHM-behr

### DECEMBER

December
**der Dezember**
dehr deh-TSEHM-behr

| in July | **im Juli** | ihm YOO-lee |
| since September | **seit September** | ziet zehp-TEHM-behr |
| until October | **bis Oktober** | bihs ohk-TOH-behr |
| for two months | **zwei Monate lang** | tsvie MOH-nah-teh lahnk |

| | | | | | |
|---|---|---|---|---|---|
| morning | late morning | noon | afternoon | evening | night |
| **der Morgen** | **der Vormittag** | **der Mittag** | **der Nachmittag** | **der Abend** | **die Nacht** |
| dehr MOHR-gehn | dehr FOHR-mih-tahk | dehr mih-tahk | dehr NAHKH-mih-tahk | dehr AH-behnt | dee nahkht |

| | | |
|---|---|---|
| in the morning | **am Morgen** | ahm MOHR-gehn |
| in the evening | **am Abend** | ahm AH-behnt |
| in the night | **in der Nacht** | ihn dehr nahkht |

cash
**das Bargeld**
dahs BAHR-gehlt

ATM / cashpoint
**der Geldautomat**
dehr GEHLT-ow-toh-maht

bank statement
**der Kontoauszug**
dehr KOHN-toh-ows-tsook

cheque
**der Scheck**
dehr shehk

| | | |
|---|---|---|
| account | **das Konto** | dahs KOHN-toh |
| bank | **die Bank** | dee bahnk |
| bank charges | **die Bankgebühren** | dee BAHNK-geh-bew-rehn |
| debit card | **die Debitkarte** | dee DEH-beet-kahr-tuh |
| debt | **die Schulden** | dee SHOOL-dehn |
| current account | **das Sparkonto** | dahs SHPAHR-kohn-toh |
| loan | **das Darlehen** | dahs DAHR-leh-uhn |
| mortgage | **die Hypothek** | dee hew-poh-TEHK |
| savings account | **die Ersparnisse** | dee ehr-SHPAHR-nih-seh |
| standing order | **der Dauerauftrag** | dehr DO-wehr-owf-trahk |
| to borrow money | **Geld ausleihen** | gehlt OWS-lah-yehn |
| to invest | **investieren** | ihn-vehs-TEE-rehn |
| to lend money | **Geld leihen** | gehlt LIE-yehn |
| to pay | **bezahlen** | beh-TSAH-lehn |
| to take out a loan | **ein Darlehen aufnehmen** | ien DAHR-leh-uhn OWF-neh-mehn |
| to withdraw from the account | **vom Konto abheben** | fohm KOHN-toh AHP-heh-behn |
| to take out a mortgage | **eine Hypothek aufnehmen** | IE-nuh hew-poh-TEHK OWF-neh-mehn |
| to withdraw | **abheben** | AHP-heh-behn |

credit card
**die Kreditkarte**
dee kreh-DEET-kahr-tuh

to save
**sparen**
SHPAH-rehn

Pound Sterling
**der Pfund Sterling**
dehr PFOONT
SHTEHR-lihnk

Euro
**der Euro**
dehr OY-roh

Dollar
**der Dollar**
dehr DOH-lahr

Franc
**der Franc**
dehr frahnk

Yen
**der Yen**
dehr yehn

Won
**der Won**
dehr vohn

Yuan
**der Yuan**
dehr YOO-ahn

Indian Rupee
**die Indische Rupie**
dee IHN-dih-shuh
ROO-peeuh

Zloty
**der Zloty**
dehr ZLOH-tee

Ruble
**der Rubel**
dehr ROO-behl

Leu
**der Leu**
dehr loy

Forint
**der Forint**
dehr FOH-rihnt

| | | |
|---|---|---|
| Krone | **die Krone** | dih KROH-neh |
| Peso | **der Peso** | dehr PEH-zoh |
| Pound | **der Pfund** | dehr pfoont |
| Dinar | **der Dinar** | dehr dee-NAHR |
| Shilling | **der Schilling** | dehr SHIH-lihnk |
| Won | **der Won** | dehr vohn |
| Dirham | **der Dirham** | dehr DEER-hahm |
| Rial | **der Rial** | dehr REE-yahl |
| Dong | **der Dong** | dehr dohng |

| | | |
|---|---|---|
| exchange rate | **die Tauschrate** | dee TOWSH-rah-tuh |
| exchange rate for US Dollars to Japanese Yen | **der Wechselkurs für US-Dollar und Japanische Yen** | dehr VEHK-sehl-koors fewr oo-EHS-DOH-lahr unt yah-PAH-nih-shuh yehn |
| foreign exchange | **die Devisen** | dee deh-VEE-zehn |
| foreign exchange rate | **der Wechselkurs** | dehr VEHK-sehl-koors |

 PEOPLE

a middle-aged man
**ein Mann mittleren Alters**
ien mahn MIHT-leh-rehn
AHL-tehrs

an old man
**ein alter Mann**
ien AHL-tehr
mahn

a young man
**ein junger Mann**
ien YOON-gehr mahn

a young woman
**eine junge Frau**
IE-nuh YOON-guh frow

baby
**das Baby**
dahs BEH-bee

a teenage boy
**ein Teenager**
ien TEE-neh-gehr

a young boy
**ein kleiner Junge**
ien KLIE-nehr
YOON-guh

a teenage girl
**ein junges Mädchen**
ien YOON-gehs MEHT-shehn

| | | |
|---|---|---|
| teenager | **der Teenager** | dehr TEE-neh-gehr |
| a young girl | **ein junges Mädchen** | ien YOON-gehs MEHT-shehn |
| a seven-year-old girl | **ein sieben Jahre altes Mädchen** | ien ZEE-behn YAH-ruh AHL-tehs MEHT-shehn |
| young | **jung** | yoonk |
| middle-aged | **mittleren Alters** | MIHT-leh-rehn AHL-tehrs |
| old | **alt** | ahlt |
| adult | **erwachsen** | ehr-VAHK-sehn |
| She is forty years old. | **Sie ist vierzig Jahre alt.** | zee ihst FEER-tsihk YAH-ruh ahlt |
| She is in her thirties. | **Sie ist in den Dreißigern.** | zee ihst ihn dehn DRIE-see-gehrn |
| She is about twenty. | **Sie ist etwa zwanzig.** | zee ihst EHT-fah TSVAHN-tsihk |
| child | **das Kind** | dahs kihnt |
| a little boy | **ein kleiner Junge** | ien KLIE-nehr YOON-guh |
| a little girl | **ein kleines Mädchen** | ien KLIE-nehs MEHT-shehn |
| He is six years old. | **Er ist sechs Jahre alt.** | ehr ihst zehks YAH-ruh ahlt |

a beautiful girl
**ein schönes Mädchen**
ien SHERH-nehs MEHT-shehn

a pretty woman
**eine hübsche Frau**
IE-nuh HEWP-shuh frow

a handsome man
**ein stattlicher Mann**
ien SHTAHT-lee-shehr mahn

| | | | | | |
|---|---|---|---|---|---|
| attractive | **attraktiv** | ah-trahk-TEEF | dirty | **dreckig** | DREH-kihk |
| beautiful | **schön** | shern | elegant | **elegant** | eh-leh-GAHNT |
| cute | **niedlich** | NEET-leesh | fashionable | **modisch** | MOH-dihsh |
| handsome | **gut aussehend** | goot OWS-seh-ehnt | neat | **ordentlich** | OHR-dehnt-lihsh |
| pretty | **hübsch** | hewpsh | poorly dressed | **schlecht gekleidet** | shlehsht geh-KLIE-deht |
| ugly | **hässlich** | HEHS-lihsh | untidy | **unordentlich** | OON-ohr-dehnt-lihsh |
| unattractive | **unattraktiv** | OON-ah-trahk-teef | well-dressed | **gut angezogen** | goot AHN-ge-tsoh-gehn |
| casually dressed | **lässig gekleidet** | LEH-sihk geh-KLIE-deht | | | |

| She is taller than him. | **Sie ist größer als er.** | zee ihst GRER-sehr ahls ehr |
| He isn't as tall as her. | **Er ist nicht so groß wie sie.** | ehr ihst nihsht zoh grohs vee zee |
| She is of average height. | **Sie ist durchschnittlich groß.** | zee ihst DOORSH-shniht-lihsh grohs |

| very tall | tall | quite tall | not very tall | short |
|---|---|---|---|---|
| **sehr groß** | **groß** | **ziemlich groß** | **nicht sehr groß** | **klein** |
| zehr grohs | grohs | TSEEM-lihsh grohs | nihkst zehr grohs | klien |

| thin | slim | plump | fat |
|------|------|-------|-----|
| **dünn** | **schlank** | **rundlich** | **fett** |
| dewn | shlahnk | ROONT-lihsh | feht |

| slender | **mager** | MAH-gehr |
|---------|-----------|----------|
| skinny | **abgemagert** | AHP-geh-mah-gehrt |
| obese | **fettleibig** | FEHT-lie-bihk |
| underweight | **das Untergewicht** | dahs OON-tehr-geh-vihsht |
| overweight | **das Übergewicht** | dahs EW-behr-geh-vihsht |
| She is overweight / underweight. | **Sie ist übergewichtig / untergewichtig.** | zee ihst EW-behr-geh-vihsh-tihk / OON-tehr-geh-vihsh-tihk |
| to lose weight | **das Gewicht verlieren** | dahs geh-VIHSHT fehr-LEE-rehn |

grey
**grau**
grow

red
**rot**
roht

dark
**dunkel**
DOON-kehl

black
**schwarz**
shvarts

blond
**blond**
blohnt

light
**hell**
hehl

chestnut
**kastanienbraun**
kahs-TAH-neeuhn-brown

brown
**braun**
brown

| straight | curly | wavy | thick | bald |
|---|---|---|---|---|
| **glatt** | **lockig** | **wellig** | **dick** | **kahl** |
| glaht | LOH-kihk | VEH-lihk | deek | kahl |

| long | short | shoulder-length | medium-length |
|---|---|---|---|
| **lang** | **kurz** | **Schulterlänge** | **mittlere Länge** |
| lahnk | koorts | SHOOL-tehr-lehn-guh | MIHT-leh-ruh LEHN-guh |

| a brunette | **eine Brünette** | IE-nuh brew-NEH-tuh |
|---|---|---|
| a redhead | **eine Rothaarige** | IE-nuh ROHT-hah-ree-guh |
| a blonde | **eine Blondine** | IE-nuh blohn-DEE-nuh |
| a dark-haired woman | **eine dunkelhaarige Frau** | IE-nuh DOON-kehl-hah-ree-guh frow |
| He has long dark hair. | **Er hat lange dunkle Haare.** | ehr haht LAHN-guh DOON-kluh HAH-ruh |
| He has curly hair. | **Er hat lockiges Haar.** | ehr haht LOH-kee-gehs hahr |
| He is bald. | **Er ist glatzköpfig.** | ehr ihst GLAHTS-kerp-fihk |

eyebrows
**die Augenbrauen**
dee OW-gehn-bro-wehn

eyelashes
**die Wimpern**
dee VIHM-pehrn

glasses
**die Brille**
dee BRIH-luh

sunglasses
**die Sonnenbrille**
dee ZOH-nehn-brih-luh

| | | |
|---|---|---|
| blue | **blau** | blow |
| grey | **grau** | grow |
| green | **grün** | grewn |
| brown | **braun** | brown |
| dark | **dunkel** | DOON-kehl |
| light | **hell** | hehl |

| | | |
|---|---|---|
| short sighted | **kurzsichtig** | KOORTS-zihsh-tihk |
| blind | **blind** | blihnt |
| She wears glasses. | **Sie trägt eine Brille.** | zee trehkt IE-nuh BRIH-luh |
| She has blue eyes. | **Sie hat blaue Augen.** | zee haht BLO-wuh OW-gehn |
| His eyes are dark brown. | **Seine Augen sind dunkelbraun.** | ZIE-nuh OW-gehn zihnt DOON-kehl-brown |

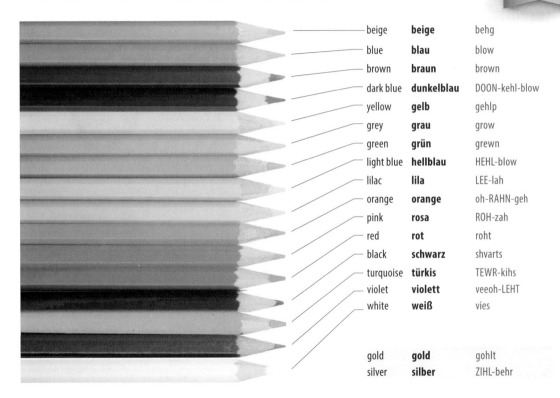

| beige | **beige** | behg |
| blue | **blau** | blow |
| brown | **braun** | brown |
| dark blue | **dunkelblau** | DOON-kehl-blow |
| yellow | **gelb** | gehlp |
| grey | **grau** | grow |
| green | **grün** | grewn |
| light blue | **hellblau** | HEHL-blow |
| lilac | **lila** | LEE-lah |
| orange | **orange** | oh-RAHN-geh |
| pink | **rosa** | ROH-zah |
| red | **rot** | roht |
| black | **schwarz** | shvarts |
| turquoise | **türkis** | TEWR-kihs |
| violet | **violett** | veeoh-LEHT |
| white | **weiß** | vies |
| | | |
| gold | **gold** | gohlt |
| silver | **silber** | ZIHL-behr |

positive
**positiv**
POH-zee-teef

stubborn
**stur**
shtoor

lucky
**glücklich**
GLEWK-lihk

dreamer
**der Träumer**
dehr TROY-mehr

visionary
**visionär**
vee-zeeoh-NEHR

funny
**lustig**
LOOS-tihk

talkative
**gesprächig**
geh-SHPREH-khihk

energetic
**energisch**
eh-NEHR-gihsh

negative
**negativ**
NEH-gah-teef

| creative | **kreativ** | kreh-ah-TEEF |
| adventurous | **abenteuerlich** | AH-behn-to-yehr-lihsh |
| kind | **nett** | neht |
| calm | **ruhig** | ROO-eek |
| caring | **fürsorglich** | FEWR-zohr-glihsh |
| punctual | **pünktlich** | PEWNKT-lihsh |
| crazy | **verrückt** | fehr-REWKT |
| liar | **der Lügner** | dehr LEWK-nehr |
| frank | **aufrichtig** | OWF-rihsh-tihk |
| strong | **stark** | shtahrk |

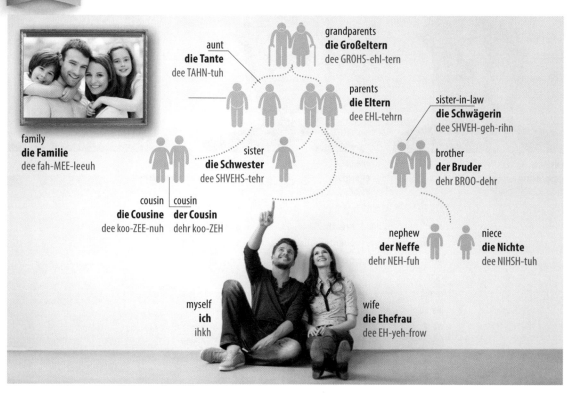

grandparents
**die Großeltern**
dee GROHS-ehl-tern

aunt
**die Tante**
dee TAHN-tuh

parents
**die Eltern**
dee EHL-tehrn

sister-in-law
**die Schwägerin**
dee SHVEH-geh-rihn

family
**die Familie**
dee fah-MEE-leeuh

sister
**die Schwester**
dee SHVEHS-tehr

brother
**der Bruder**
dehr BROO-dehr

cousin
**die Cousine**
dee koo-ZEE-nuh

cousin
**der Cousin**
dehr koo-ZEH

nephew
**der Neffe**
dehr NEH-fuh

niece
**die Nichte**
dee NIHSH-tuh

myself
**ich**
ihkh

wife
**die Ehefrau**
dee EH-yeh-frow

| | | |
|---|---|---|
| grandchildren | **die Enkelkinder** | dee EHN-kehl-kihn-dehr |
| daughter | **die Tochter** | dee TOHKH-tehr |
| father | **der Vater** | dehr FAH-tehr |
| father-in-law | **der Schwiegervater** | dehr SHVEE-gehr-fah-tehr |
| grandchild | **der Enkel** | dehr EHN-kehl |
| granddaughter | **die Enkelin** | dee EHN-keh-lihn |
| grandson | **der Enkel** | dehr EHN-kehl |
| grandfather | **der Großvater** | dehr GROHS-fah-tehr |
| grandmother | **die Großmutter** | dee GROHS-moo-tehr |
| great-grandparents | **die Urgroßeltern** | dee OOR-grohs-ehl-tehrn |
| husband | **der Ehemann** | dehr EH-yeh-mahn |
| mother | **die Mutter** | dee MOO-tehr |
| mother-in-law | **die Schwiegermutter** | dee SHVEE-gehr-moo-tehr |
| son | **der Sohn** | dehr zohn |
| twin brother | **der Zwillingsbruder** | dehr TSVIH-lihnks-broo-dehr |
| brother-in-law | **der Schwager** | dehr SHVAH-gehr |

single child
**das Einzelkind**
dahs IEN-tsehl-kihnt

family with two children
**die Familie mit zwei Kindern**
dee fah-MEE-leeuh miht tsvie KIHN-dehrn

big family
**die Großfamilie**
dee GROHS-fah-mee-leeuh

childless
**kinderlos**
KIHN-dehr-lohs

single father
**der alleinerziehende Vater**
dehr ah-LIEN-ehr-tsee-yehn-duh FAH-tehr

single mother
**die alleinerziehende Mutter**
dee ah-LIEN-ehr-tsee-yehn-duh MOO-tehr

adoption
**die Adoption**
dee ah-dohp-TSEEOHN

orphan
**die Waise**
dee VIE-zuh

widow
**die Witwe**
dee VIHT-fuh

| | | |
|---|---|---|
| stepfather | **der Stiefvater** | dehr SHTEEF-fah-tehr |
| stepmother | **die Stiefmutter** | dee SHTEEHF-moo-tehr |
| to be pregnant | **schwanger sein** | SHVAN-gehr zien |
| to expect a baby | **ein Baby erwarten** | ien BEH-bee ehr-VAHR-tehn |
| to give birth to | **gebären** | geh-BEH-rehn |
| born | **geboren** | geh-BOH-rehn |
| to baptise | **taufen** | TOW-fehn |
| to raise | **erziehen** | ehr-TSEE-yehn |

| | | |
|---|---|---|
| to be engaged | **verlobt sein** | vehr-LOHPT zien |
| to marry | **heiraten** | HIE-rah-tehn |
| to be married to | **verheiratet sein mit** | vehr-HIE-rah-teht zien miht |
| divorced | **geschieden** | geh-SHEE-dehn |
| widowed | **verwitwet** | fehr-VIHT-feht |
| widow | **die Witwe** | dee VIHT-fuh |
| widower | **der Witwer** | dehr VIHT-fehr |
| to die | **sterben** | SHTEHR-behn |

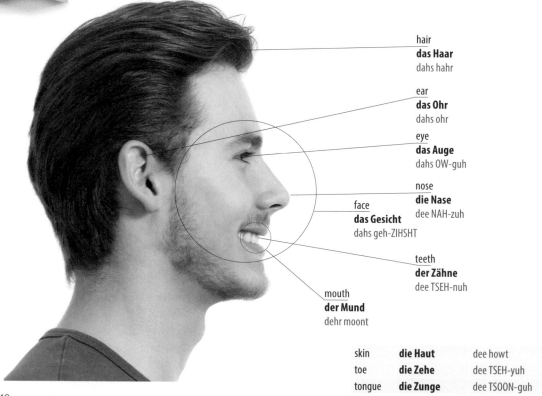

hair
**das Haar**
dahs hahr

ear
**das Ohr**
dahs ohr

eye
**das Auge**
dahs OW-guh

nose
**die Nase**
dee NAH-zuh

face
**das Gesicht**
dahs geh-ZIHSHT

teeth
**der Zähne**
dee TSEH-nuh

mouth
**der Mund**
dehr moont

| skin | **die Haut** | dee howt |
| toe | **die Zehe** | dee TSEH-yuh |
| tongue | **die Zunge** | dee TSOON-guh |

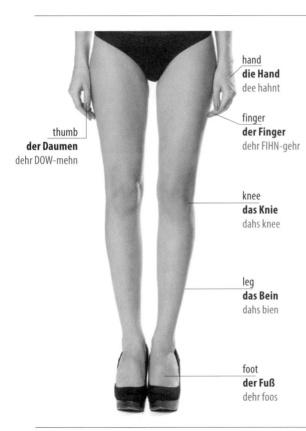

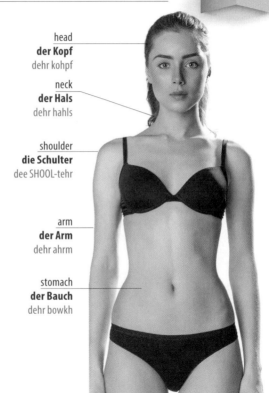

hand
**die Hand**
dee hahnt

finger
**der Finger**
dehr FIHN-gehr

thumb
**der Daumen**
dehr DOW-mehn

knee
**das Knie**
dahs knee

leg
**das Bein**
dahs bien

foot
**der Fuß**
dehr foos

head
**der Kopf**
dehr kohpf

neck
**der Hals**
dehr hahls

shoulder
**die Schulter**
dee SHOOL-tehr

arm
**der Arm**
dehr ahrm

stomach
**der Bauch**
dehr bowkh

angry
**wütend**
VEW-tehnt

annoyed
**verärgert**
vehr-EHR-gehrt

ashamed
**beschämt**
beh-SHEHMT

betrayed
**verraten**
fehr-RAH-tehn

confused
**verwirrt**
fehr-VIHRT

confident
**zuversichtlich**
TSOO-vehr-zihsht-lihsh

cheated
**betrogen**
beh-TROH-gehn

depressed
**gedrückt**
geh-DREWKT

delighted
**erfreut**
ehr-FROYT

disappointed
**enttäuscht**
ehnt-TOYSHT

excited
**aufgeregt**
OWF-geh-rehkt

embarrassed
**verlegen**
fehr-LEH-gehn

furious
**wütend**
VEW-tehnt

frightened
**erschrocken**
ehr-SHROH-kehn

happy
**glücklich**
GLEWK-lihsh

horrified
**entsetzt**
ehnt-ZEHTST

irritated
**irritiert**
ee-ree-TEERT

intrigued
**fasziniert**
fahs-tsee-NEERT

jealous
**eifersüchtig**
IE-fehr-zeskh-tihk

lazy
**faul**
fowl

lucky
**glücklich**
GLEWK-lihsh

relaxed
**entspannt**
ehnt-SHPAHNT

sad
**traurig**
TROW-rihk

stressed
**gestresst**
ge-SHTREHST

terrified
**erschrocken**
ehr-SHROH-kehn

upset
**verärgert**
fehr-EHR-gehrt

unhappy
**unzufrieden**
OON-tsoo-free-dehn

| | | | |
|---|---|---|---|
| hobby **das Hobby** dahs HOH-bee | My hobby is . . . Are you interested in . . .? | **Mein Hobby ist . . .** **Interessierts du dich /** **Interessieren Sie sich für . . .?** | mien HOH-bee ihst ... ihn-teh-reh-SEERST doo dihsh / ihn-teh- reh-SEE-rehn zee zihsh fewr ...? |

baking
**das Backen**
dahs BAH-kehn

coin collecting
**das Münzensammeln**
dahs MEWN-tsehn-zah-mehln

woodworking
**die Holzverarbeitung**
dee HOHLTS-fehr-ahr-bie-toonk

stamp collecting
**das Briefmarkensammeln**
dahs BREEF-mahr-kehn-zah-mehln

cooking
**das Kochen**
dahs KOH-khehn

dance
**das Tanzen**
dahs TAHN-tsehn

drawing
**das Zeichnen**
dahs TSIE-shehn

reading
**das Lesen**
dahs LEH-zehn

jewellery making
**das Schmuckmachen**
dahs SHMOOK-mah-khehn

knitting
**das Stricken**
dahs SHTRIH-kehn

painting
**das Malen**
dahs MAH-lehn

sewing
**das Nähen**
dahs NEH-yehn

badminton
**das Badminton**
dahs BEHT-mihn-tohn

bowling
**das Bowling**
dahs BOW-lihnk

boxing
**das Boxen**
dahs BOH-xehn

chess
**das Schach**
dahs shahkh

cycling
**das Radfahren**
dahs RAHT-fah-rehn

darts
**das Darts**
dahs dahrts

**02**

diving
**das Tauchen**
dahs TOW-khehn

fishing
**das Angeln**
dahs AHN-gehln

football
**der Fußball**
dehr FOOS-bahl

orienteering
**das Geocaching**
dahs GEH-oh-kay-cheenk

gymnastics
**die Gymnastik**
dee gewm-NAHS-tihk

handball
**der Handball**
dehr HAHNT-bahl

jogging
**das Jogging**
dahs GOH-gihnk

kayaking
**das Kayaking**
dahs KAH-yah-kihnk

martial arts
**der Kampfsport**
dehr KAHMPF-shpohrt

mountain biking
**das Mountainbiking**
dahs MOWN-tehn-bie-kihnk

paintball
**der Paintball**
dehr PEHNT-bohl

photography
**die Fotografie**
dee foh-toh-grah-FEE

rock climbing
**das Felsklettern**
dahs FEHLS-kleh-tehrn

running
**das Laufen**
dahs LOW-fehn

sailing
**das Segeln**
dahs ZEH-gehln

surfing
**das Surfen**
dahs ZEHR-fehn

swimming
**das Schwimmen**
dahs SHVIH-mehn

table tennis
**das Tischtennis**
dahs TIHSH-teh-nihs

travel
**das Reisen**
dahs RIE-zehn

tennis
**das Tennis**
dahs TEH-nihs

yoga
**das Yoga**
dahs YOH-gah

I like to swim.   **Ich schwimme gern.**   ihsh SHVIH-muh gehrn

What activities do you like to do?   **Was machst du / machen Sie gern?**   vahs mahkhst doo / MAH-khehn zee gehrn?

to get up
**aufstehen**
OWF-shteh-yehn

to take a shower
**duschen**
DOO-shehn

to brush your teeth
**die Zähne putzen**
dee TSEH-nuh POO-tsehn

to floss your teeth
**die Zähne mit der Zahnseide reinigen**
dee TSEH-nuh miht dehr TSAHN-zie-duh
RIE-nee-gehn

to shave
**rasieren**
rah-ZEE-rehn

to brush your hair
**das Haar bürsten**
dahs HAHR BEWR-stehn

to put on makeup
**sich schminken**
zihsh SHMIHN-kehn

to get dressed
**sich anziehen**
zihsh AHN-tsee-yehn

to get undressed
**sich ausziehen**
zihsh OWS-tsee-yehn

to take a bath
**baden**
BAH-dehn

to go to bed
**zu Bett gehen**
tsoo beht GEH-ehn

to sleep
**schlafen**
SHLAH-fehn

Valentine's Day
**der Valentinstag**
dehr VAH-lehn-teens-tahk

graduation
**der Schulabschluss**
dehr SHOOL-ahp-shloos

Easter
**das Ostern**
dahs OHS-tehrn

engagement
**die Verlobung**
dee fehr-LOH-boonk

marriage
**die Heirat**
dee HIE-raht

bride
**die Braut**
dee browt

Christmas
**das Weihnachten**
dahs VIE-nahkh-tehn

Santa Claus / Father Christmas
**der Weihnachtsmann**
dehr VIE-nahkhts-mahn

candle
**die Kerze**
dee KEHR-tsuh

present / gift
**das Geschenk**
dahs geh-SHEHNK

Advent calendar
**der Adventskalender**
dehr ahd-VEHNTS-kah-lehn-dehr

decoration
**die Dekoration**
dee deh-koh-rah-TSEEOHN

champagne
**der Champagner**
dehr sham-PAH-nee-yehr

party
**die Party**
dee PAHR-tee

mistletoe
**die Mistel**
dee MIHS-tehl

fireworks
**das Feuerwerk**
dahs FO-yehr-vehrk

birthday
**der Geburtstag**
dehr geh-BOORTS-tahk

ceremony
**die Zeremonie**
dee tseh-reh-moh-NEE

wedding ring
**der Ehering**
dehr EH-yeh-rihnk

decorated eggs
**die Ostereier**
dee OHS-tehr-ier

Easter Bunny
**der Osterhase**
dehr OHS-tehr-hah-zuh

| | | |
|---|---|---|
| Happy New Year! | **Frohes neues Jahr!** | FROH-ehs NOH-yehs yahr! |
| Happy Birthday! | **Alles Gute zum Geburtstag!** | AH-lehs GOO-tuh tsoom geh-BOORTS-tahk! |
| All the best! | **Alles Gute!** | AH-lehs GOO-tuh! |
| Good luck! | **Viel Glück!** | Feel glewk! |

| | | |
|---|---|---|
| Congratulations! | **Herzliche Glückwünsche!** | HEHRTS-lee-shuh GLEWK-vewn-shuh! |
| Merry Christmas! | **Fröhliche Weihnachten!** | FRER-lee-shuh VIE-nahkh-tehn! |
| Happy Easter! | **Frohe Ostern!** | FROH-uh OHS-tehrn! |
| New Year | **das Neujahr** | dahs NOY-yahr |

Christianity
**das Christentum**
dahs KRIHS-tehn-toom

Confucianism
**der Konfuzianismus**
dehr kohn-foo-tsee-yah-NIHS-moos

Jainism
**der Jainismus**
dehr yah-ee-NIHS-moos

Islam
**der Islam**
dehr ihs-LAHM

Buddhism
**der Buddhismus**
dehr boot-DIHS-moos

Judaism
**das Judentum**
dahs YOO-dehn-toom

Hinduism
**der Hinduismus**
dehr hihn-doo-IHS-moos

Taoism
**der Taoismus**
dehr tah-oh-IHS-moos

Sikhism
**der Sikhismus**
dehr zihk-HIHS-moos

| | | |
|---|---|---|
| to confess | **sich bekennen zu** | zihsh beh-KEH-nehn tsoo |
| without religious confession | **ohne religiöses Bekenntnis** | OH-nuh reh-lee-GER-zehs beh-KEHNT-nihs |
| to believe in God | **an Gott glauben** | ahn goht GLOW-behn |
| to have faith | **gläubig sein** | GLOY-bihk zien |
| to pray | **beten** | BEH-tehn |

# HOME & HOUSEKEEPING

house
**das Haus**
dahs hows

flat
**die Wohnung**
dee VOH-noonk

block of flats
**der Wohnblock**
dehr VOHN-blohk

duplex / two-storey house
**zweistöckiges Doppelhaus**
TSVIE-shter-kee-gehs DOH-pehl-hows

detached house
**das Einfamilienhaus**
dahs IEN-fah-mee-leeuhn-hows

co-ownership
**das Miteigentum**
dahs MIHT-ie-gehn-toom

houseboat
**das Hausboot**
dahs HOWS-boot

farm
**der Bauernhof**
dehr BO-wern-hohf

caravan
**der Wohnwagen**
dehr VOHN-vah-gehn

flatshare
**die Wohngemeinschaft**
dee VOHN-geh-mien-shahft

| Where do you live? | **Wo wohnst du / wohnen Sie?** | voo vohnst doo / VOH-nehn zee? |
|---|---|---|
| I live in a flatshare. | **Ich wohne in einer WG.** | ihsh VOH-nuh in IE-nehr VEH-GEH |
| I live with my parents. | **Ich wohne bei meinen Eltern.** | ihsh VOH-nuh bie MIE-nehn EHL-tehrn |

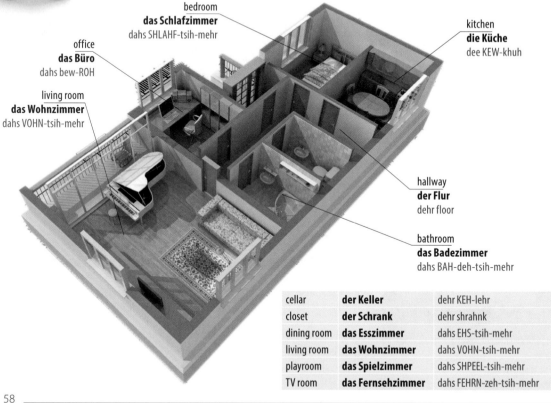

bedroom
**das Schlafzimmer**
dahs SHLAHF-tsih-mehr

kitchen
**die Küche**
dee KEW-khuh

office
**das Büro**
dahs bew-ROH

living room
**das Wohnzimmer**
dahs VOHN-tsih-mehr

hallway
**der Flur**
dehr floor

bathroom
**das Badezimmer**
dahs BAH-deh-tsih-mehr

| cellar | **der Keller** | dehr KEH-lehr |
|---|---|---|
| closet | **der Schrank** | dehr shrahnk |
| dining room | **das Esszimmer** | dahs EHS-tsih-mehr |
| living room | **das Wohnzimmer** | dahs VOHN-tsih-mehr |
| playroom | **das Spielzimmer** | dahs SHPEEL-tsih-mehr |
| TV room | **das Fernsehzimmer** | dahs FEHRN-zeh-tsih-mehr |

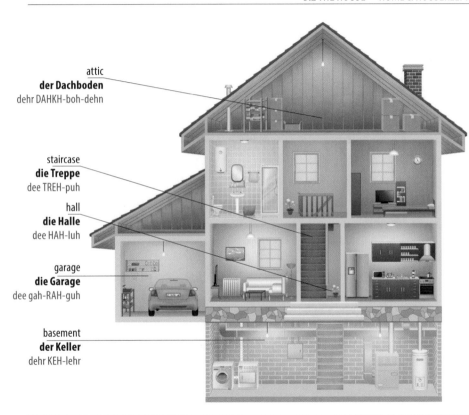

attic
**der Dachboden**
dehr DAHKH-boh-dehn

staircase
**die Treppe**
dee TREH-puh

hall
**die Halle**
dee HAH-luh

garage
**die Garage**
dee gah-RAH-guh

basement
**der Keller**
dehr KEH-lehr

porch
**die Veranda**
dee veh-RAHN-dah

patio
**die Terrasse**
dee teh-RAH-suh

workshop
**die Werkstatt**
dee VEHRK-shtaht

window
**das Fenster**
dahs FEHNS-tehr

bed
**das Bett**
dahs beht

lamp
**die Lampe**
dee LAHM-puh

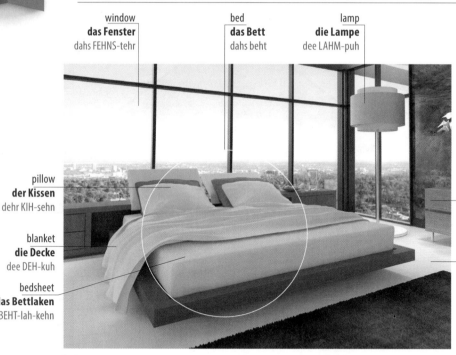

pillow
**der Kissen**
dehr KIH-sehn

blanket
**die Decke**
dee DEH-kuh

bedsheet
**das Bettlaken**
dahs BEHT-lah-kehn

chest of drawers
**die Kommode**
dee koh-MOH-duh

carpet
**der Teppichboden**
dehr TEH-pihsch-boh-dehn

bedroom
**das Schlafzimmer**
dahs SHLAHF-tsih-mehr

bed linen **die Bettwäsche** dee BEHT-veh-shuh

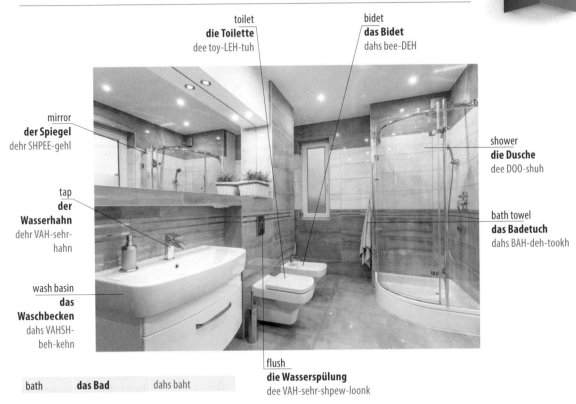

toilet
**die Toilette**
dee toy-LEH-tuh

bidet
**das Bidet**
dahs bee-DEH

mirror
**der Spiegel**
dehr SHPEE-gehl

shower
**die Dusche**
dee DOO-shuh

tap
**der Wasserhahn**
dehr VAH-sehr-hahn

bath towel
**das Badetuch**
dahs BAH-deh-tookh

wash basin
**das Waschbecken**
dahs VAHSH-beh-kehn

flush
**die Wasserspülung**
dee VAH-sehr-shpew-loonk

bath    **das Bad**    dahs baht

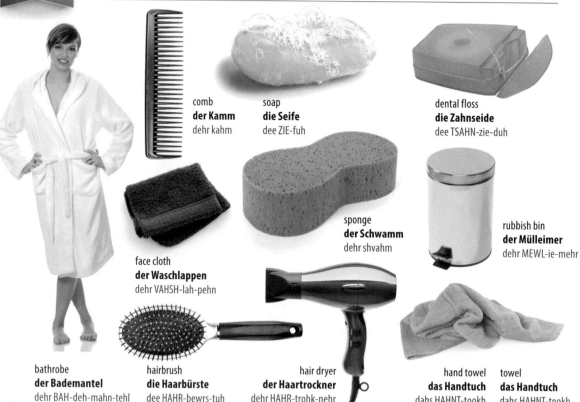

comb
**der Kamm**
dehr kahm

soap
**die Seife**
dee ZIE-fuh

dental floss
**die Zahnseide**
dee TSAHN-zie-duh

sponge
**der Schwamm**
dehr shvahm

rubbish bin
**der Mülleimer**
dehr MEWL-ie-mehr

face cloth
**der Waschlappen**
dehr VAHSH-lah-pehn

bathrobe
**der Bademantel**
dehr BAH-deh-mahn-tehl

hairbrush
**die Haarbürste**
dee HAHR-bewrs-tuh

hair dryer
**der Haartrockner**
dehr HAHR-trohk-nehr

hand towel
**das Handtuch**
dahs HAHNT-tookh

towel
**das Handtuch**
dahs HAHNT-tookh

shaving cream
**der Rasierschaum**
dehr rah-ZEER-showm

toothbrush
**die Zahnbürste**
dee TSAHN-bewrs-tuh

razor
**der Rasierer**
dehr rah-ZEE-rehr

shampoo
**das Shampoo**
dahs shahm-POO

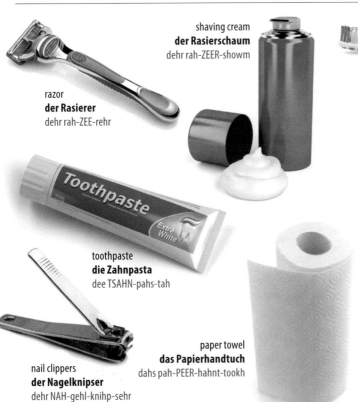

conditioner
**die Haarkur**
dee HAHR-koor

toothpaste
**die Zahnpasta**
dee TSAHN-pahs-tah

nail clippers
**der Nagelknipser**
dehr NAH-gehl-knihp-sehr

paper towel
**das Papierhandtuch**
dahs pah-PEER-hahnt-tookh

toilet paper
**das Toilettenpapier**
dahs toy-LEH-tehn-pah-peer

63

fridge
**der Kühlschrank**
dehr KEWL-shrahnk

microwave
**die Mikrowelle**
dee MEE-kroh-veh-luh

stove
**der Herd**
dehr hehrt

coffee machine
**die Kaffeemaschine**
dee KAH-feh-mah-
shee-nuh

freezer
**der Gefrierschrank**
dehr geh-FREER-shrahnk

washing machine
**die Waschmaschine**
dee VAHSH-mah-shee-nuh

oven
**der Ofen**
dehr OH-fehn

dishwasher
**der Geschirrspüler**
dehr geh-SHIHR-shpew-lehr

kettle
**der Wasserkocher**
dehr VAH-sehr-koh-khehr

toaster
**der Toaster**
dehr TOWS-tehr

cookery book
**das Kochbuch**
dahs KOHKH-bookh

dishcloth
**das Abwaschtuch**
dahs AHP-vahsh-tookh

draining board
**der Geschirrabtropfer**
dehr geh-SHIHR-ahp-trohp-fehr

kitchen roll
**die Küchenrolle**
dee KEW-shehn-roh-luh

plug
**der Stöpsel**
dehr SHTERP-sehl

tea towel
**das Geschirrtuch**
dahs geh-SHIHR-tookh

shelf
**das Regal**
dahs reh-GAHL

sink
**das Spülbecken**
dahs SHPEWL-beh-kehn

tablecloth
**die Tischdecke**
dee TIHSH-deh-kuh

bottle opener
**der Flaschenöffner**
dehr FLAH-shehn-erf-nehr

chopping board
**das Hackbrett**
dahs HAHK-breht

colander
**der Sieb / der Seiher**
dehr zeep / dehr ZIE-yehr

frying pan
**die Pfanne**
dee PFAH-nuh

grater
**die Reibe**
dee RIE-buh

juicer
**der Entsafter**
dehr ehnt-ZAHF-tehr

corkscrew
**der Korkenzieher**
dehr KOHR-kehn-tsee-yehr

kitchen scales
**die Küchenwaage**
dee KEW-ksehn-vah-guh

mixing bowl
**die Rührschüssel**
dee REWR-shew-sehl

sieve
**der Sieb**
dehr zeep

saucepan
**der Topf**
dehr tohpf

whisk
**der Schneebesen**
dehr SHNEE-beh-zehn

tin opener
**der Dosenöffner**
dehr DOH-zehn-erf-nehr

washing-up liquid
**das Geschirrspülmittel**
dahs geh-SHIHR-shpewl-mih-tehl

| to do the dishes / to do the washing up | **das Geschirr spülen** | dahs geh-SHIHR SHPEW-lehn |
| to do the washing | **den Abwasch erledigen** | dehn AHP-vahsh ehr-LEH-dee-gehn |
| to clear the table | **den Tisch abräumen** | dehn TIHSH AHP-roy-mehn |
| to set the table | **den Tisch decken** | dehn TIHSH DEH-kehn |

| | | |
|---|---|---|
| cutlery | **das Besteck** | dahs beh-SHTEHK |
| soup spoon | **der Suppenlöffel** | dehr ZOO-pehn-ler-fehl |
| spoon | **der Löffel** | dehr LER-fehl |

tablespoon
**der Esslöffel**
dehr EHS-ler-fehl

fork
**die Gabel**
dee GAH-behl

knife
**das Messer**
dahs MEH-sehr

teaspoon
**der Teelöffel**
dehr TEH-ler-fehl

coffee spoon
**der Kaffeelöffel**
dehr KAH-feh-ler-fehl

plate
**der Teller**
dehr TEH-lehr

mug
**der Becher**
dehr BEH-ksehr

sugar dispenser
**der Zuckerstreuer**
dehr TSOO-kehr-shtro-yehr

jug
**der Krug**
dehr krook

saucer
**die Untertasse**
dee OON-tehr-tah-suh

cup
**die Tasse**
dee TAH-suh

wine glass
**das Weinglas**
dahs VIEN-glahs

teapot
**die Teekanne**
dee TEH-kah-nuh

bowl
**die Schüssel**
dee SHEW-sehl

jar
**das Glas**
dahs glahs

| crockery | **das Geschirr** | dahs geh-SHIHR |
| glass | **das Glas** | dahs glahs |

armchair
**der Sessel**
dehr ZEH-sehl

sofa
**das Sofa**
dahs ZOH-fah

lampshade
**der Lampenschirm**
dehr LAHM-pehn-shihrm

lamp
**die Lampe**
dee LAHM-puh

vase
**die Vase**
dee VAH-zuh

rug
**der Teppich**
dehr TEH-pihsh

bookcase
**das Bücherregal**
dahs BEW-shehr-
reh-gahl

shelf
**das Regal**
dahs REH-gahl

plant
**die Pflanze**
dee PFLAHN-tsuh

picture
**das Bild**
dahs bihlt

table
**der Tisch**
dehr tihsh

chair
**der Stuhl**
dehr shtool

| I can relax here. | **Ich kann mich hier gut entspannen.** | ihsh kahn mihsh heer goot ehnt-SHPAH-nehn |
| Do you watch TV often? | **Siehst du / Sehen Sie oft fern?** | zeeyst doo / ZEH-yehn zee ohft fehrn? |
| What is the size of the living room? | **Wie groß ist das Wohnzimmer?** | vee grohs ihst dahs VOHN-tsih-mehr? |

hair dryer
**der Haartrockner**
dehr HAHR-trohk-nehr

iron
**das Bügeleisen**
dahs BEW-gehl-ie-zehn

washing machine
**die Waschmaschine**
dee VAHSH-mah-shee-nuh

radio
**das Radio**
dahs RAH-deeoh

television
**der Fernseher**
dehr FEHRN-zeh-yehr

telephone
**das Telefon**
dahs teh-leh-FOHN

cooker
**der Kochherd**
dehr kohkh-hehrt

vacuum cleaner
**der Staubsauger**
dehr SHTOWP-zow-gehr

mobile
**das Handy**
dahs HEHN-dee

microwave
**die Mikrowelle**
dee MEE-kroh-veh-luh

kettle
**der Wasserkocher**
dehr VAH-sehr-koh-khehr

refrigerator
**der Kühlschrank**
dehr KEWL-shrahnk

coffee grinder
**die Kaffeemühle**
dee KAH-feh-mew-luh

sewing machine
**die Nähmaschine**
dee NEH-mah-shee-neh

razor
**der Rasierer**
dehr rah-ZEE-rehr

blender
**der Blender**
dehr BLEHN-dehr

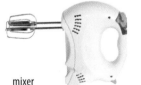

mixer
**der Mixer**
dehr MEE-xehr

gas stove
**der Gaskocher**
dehr GAHS-koh-khehr

juicer
**der Entsafter**
dehr ehnt-ZAHF-tehr

to dust
**Staub wischen**
SHTOWP VIH-shehn

to vacuum
**staubsaugen**
SHTOWP-zow-gehn

to clean the windows
**Fenster putzen**
FEHNS-tehr POO-tsehn

to clean the floor
**den Fußboden wischen**
dehn FOOS-boh-dehn VIH-shehn

to do the washing/laundry
**die Wäsche waschen**
dee VEH-shuh VAH-shehn

to do the dishes
**das Geschirr spülen**
dahs geh-SHIHR SHPEW-lehn

to clean up
**aufräumen**
OWF-roy-mehn

74

to make the bed
**das Bett machen**
dahs beht MAH-khehn

to hang up the laundry
**die Wäsche aufhängen**
dee VEH-shuh OWF-hehn-gehn

to iron
**bügeln**
BEW-gehln

bucket
**der Eimer**
dehr IE-mehr

dust cloth
**das Staubtuch**
dahs SHTOWP-tookh

feather duster
**der Staubwedel**
dehr SHTOWP-veh-dehl

dustpan
**die Schaufel**
dee SHOW-fehl

mop
**der Mopp**
dehr mohp

broom
**der Besen**
dehr BEH-zehn

clothes line
**die Wäscheleine**
dee VEH-sheh-lie-nuh

peg
**die Wäscheklammer**
dee VEH-sheh-klah-mehr

paper towels
**die Papiertücher**
dee pah-PEER-tew-khehr

laundry basket
**der Wäschekorb**
dehr VEH-sheh-kohrp

scrubbing brush
**die Bürste**
dee BEWR-stuh

window cleaner
**das Fensterputzmittel**
dahs FEHN-stehr-poots-mih-tehl

sponge
**der Schwamm**
dehr shvahm

detergent
**das Reinigungsmittel**
dahs RIE-nee-goongs-mih-tehl

| We have to clean up. | **Wir müssen aufräumen.** | veer MEW-sehn OWF-roy-mehn |
| The flat is already clean. | **Die Wohnung ist schon sauber.** | dee VOH-noonk ihst shohn ZOW-behr |
| Who does the cleaning? | **Wer macht Ordnung?** | vehr mahkht OHRD-noonk? |

# LESSONS

SCHOOL

white board
**das Whiteboard**
dahs WHITE-board

chair
**der Stuhl**
dehr shtool

book
**das Buch**
dahs bookh

table
**der Tisch**
dehr tihsh

clock
**die Uhr**
dee oor

teacher
**der Lehrer** *m* /
**die Lehrerin** *f*
dehr LEH-rehr / dee LEH-reh-rihn

student
**der Schüler** *m* / **die Schülerin** *f*
dehr SHEW-lehr /
dee SHEW-leh-rihn

tablet
**das Tablet**
dahs TAHB-leht

calculator
**der Taschenrechner**
dehr TAH-shehn-rehs-nehr

| | | | | | |
|---|---|---|---|---|---|
| to go to school | zur Schule gehen | tsoor SHOO-luh GEH-ehn | marks | die Noten | dee NOH-tehn |
| to study | studieren | shtoo-DEE-rehn | an oral exam | eine mündliche Prüfung | IE-nuh MEWNT-lee-shuh PREW-foonk |
| to learn | lernen | LEHR-nehn | a written exam | eine schriftliche Prüfung | IE-nuh SHRIHFT-lee-shuh PREW-foonk |
| to do homework | Hausaufgaben machen | HOWS-owf-gah-behn MAH-khehn | to prepare for an exam | sich auf eine Prüfung vorbereiten | zihsh owf IE-nuh PREW-foonk VOHR-beh-rie-tehn |
| to know | wissen | VIH-sehn | | | |
| to take an exam | eine Prüfung ablegen | IE-nuh PREW-foonk AHP-leh-gehn | to repeat a year | repetir un año | ien yahr vee-dehr-HOH-lehn |
| to pass | bestehen | beh-SHTE-yehn | | | |

Languages
**die Sprachen**
dee SHPRAH-khehn

Spanish
**das Spanisch**
dahs SPAH-nihsh

German
**das Deutsch**
dahs doych

English
**das Englisch**
dahs EHN-glihsh

French
**das Französisch**
dahs frahn-TSER-zihsh

Art
**die Kunst**
dee koonst

Geography
**die Erdkunde**
dee EHRT-koon-duh

Music
**die Musik**
dee moo-ZEEK

History
**die Geschichte**
dee geh-SHIHSH-tuh

Chemistry
**die Chemie**
dee sheh-MEE

Biology
**die Biologie**
dee bee-oh-loh-GEE

Mathematics
**die Mathematik**
dee mah-teh-mah-TEEK

Physical education
**der Sport**
dehr shpohrt

scissors
**die Schere**
dee SHEH-ruh

globe
**der Globus**
dehr GLOH-boos

school bag
**die Schultasche**
dee SHOOL-tah-shuh

pen
**der Kugelschreiber**
dehr KOO-gehl-shrie-behr

notebook
**das Notizbuch**
dahs noh-TEETS-bookh

pencil case
**das Federmäppchen**
dahs FEH-dehr-
mehp-shehn

ruler
**das Lineal**
dahs lee-neh-AHL

pencil
**der Bleistift**
dehr BLIE-shtihft

pencil sharpener
**der Spitzer**
dehr SHPIH-tsehr

rubber
**der Radiergummi**
dehr rah-DEER-goo-mee

highlighter
**der Markierstift**
dehr mahr-KEER-shtihft

book
**das Buch**
dahs bookh

colouring pen
**der Farbstift**
dehr FAHRP-shtihft

stapler
**der Hefter**
dehr HEHF-tehr

 WORK

job interview
**das Vorstellungsgespräch**
dahs FOHR-shteh-loongs-geh-shprehsh

recruiter
**der Personalvermittler** *m* / **die Personalvermttlerin** *f*
dehr pehr-zoh-NAHL-fehr-miht-lehr /
dee pehr-zoh-NAHL-fehr-miht-leh-rihn

candidate
**der Bewerber** *m* /
**die Bewerberin** *f*
dehr beh-VEHR-behr /
dee beh-VEHR-beh-rihn

application letter
**das Bewerbungsschreiben**
dahs beh-VEHR-boongs-
shrie-behn

CV
**der Lebenslauf**
dehr LEH-behns-lowf

| | | | | | | |
|---|---|---|---|---|---|---|
| gross | **brutto** | BROO-toh | | interview | **das Interview** | dahs ihn-tehr-VIEW |
| net | **netto** | NEH-toh | | job | **der Job** | dehr gohp |
| job advertisement | **das Stellenangebot** | dahs STEH-lehn-ahn-geh-boht | | salary | **das Gehalt** | dahs geh-HAHLT |
| application | **die Bewerbung** | dee beh-VEHR-boonk | | vacancy | **die Vakanz** | dee vah-KAHNTS |
| company | **das Unternehmen** | dahs oon-tehr-NEH-mehn | | work | **die Arbeit** | dee AHR-biet |
| education | **die Ausbildung** | dee OWS-bihl-doonk | | to hire | **anstellen** | AHN-shteh-lehn |

| | | |
|---|---|---|
| experience | **die Erfahrung** | dee ehr-FAH-roonk |
| to apply for | **sich bewerben um** | zihsh beh-VEHR-behn oom |
| assessment | **die Beurteilung** | dee beh-OOHR-tie-loonk |
| bonus | **der Bonus** | dehr BOH-noos |
| employer | **der Arbeitgeber** | dehr AHR-biet-geh-behr |
| to fire | **entlassen** | ehnt-LAH-sehn |
| fringe benefits | **die Nebenleistungen** | dee NEH-behn-lies-toon-gehn |
| maternity leave | **der Mutterschaftsurlaub** | dehr MOO-tehr-shahfts-oor-lowp |
| notice | **die Kündigung** | dee KEWN-dee-goonk |
| staff | **das Personal** | dahs pehr-zoh-NAHL |
| human resources officer | **der Personalreferent** | dehr pehr-zoh-NAHL-reh-feh-rehnt |
| promotion | **die Beförderung** | dee beh-FER-deh-roonk |
| prospects | **die Chancen** | dee SHAHN-sehn |
| to resign | **zurücktreten** | tsoo-REWK-treh-tehn |
| to retire | **in Pension gehen** | ihn pehn-ZEEOHN GEH-yehn |
| sick leave | **die Krankschreibung** | dee KRAHNK-shrie-boonk |
| strike | **der Streik** | dehr shtriek |
| trainee | **der Trainee** | dehr treh-NEE |
| training course | **die Schulung** | dee SHOO-loonk |
| unemployment benefits | **das Arbeitslosengeld** | dahs AHR-biets-loh-zehn-gehlt |
| workplace | **der Arbeitsplatz** | dehr AHR-biets-plahts |

employee
**der Mitarbeiter**
dehr MIHT-ahr-bie-tehr

actor
**der Schauspieler** *m* /
**die Schauspielerin** *f*
dehr SHOW-shpee-lehr /
dee SHOW-shpee-leh-rihn

baker
**der Bäcker** *m* /
**die Bäckerin** *f*
dehr BEH-kehr /
dee BEH-keh-rihn

banker
**der Banker** *m* /
**die Bankerin** *f*
dehr BAHN-kehr /
dee BAHN-keh-rihn

butcher
**der Metzger** *m* /
**die Metzgerin** *f*
dehr MEHTS-gehr /
dee MEHTS-geh-rihn

carpenter
**der Tischler** *m* /
**die Tischlerin** *f*
dehr TIHSH-lehr /
dee TIHSH-leh-rihn

chef
**der Koch** *m* /
**die Köchin** *f*
dehr kohkh /
dee KER-shihn

doctor
**der Arzt** *m* /
**die Ärztin** *f*
dehr ahrtst /
dee EHRTS-tihn

farmer
**der Bauer** *m* /
**die Bäuerin** *f*
dehr BO-wehr /
dee BO-yeh-rihn

fisherman
**der Fischer** *m* /
**die Fischerin** *f*
dehr FIH-shehr /
dee FIH-sheh-rihn

firefighter
**der Feuerwehrmann** *m* /
**die Feuerwehrfrau** *f*
dehr FO-yehr-vehr-mahn /
dee FO-yehr-vehr-frow

musician
**der Musiker** *m* /
**die Musikerin** *f*
dehr MOO-zee-kehr /
dee MOO-zee-keh-rihn

lawyer
**der Anwalt** *m* /
**die Anwältin** *f*
dehr AHN-vahlt /
dee AHN-vehl-tihn

nurse
**der Krankenpfleger** m /
**die Krankenschwester** f
dehr KRAHN-kehn-pfleh-gehr / dee KRAHN-kehn-shvehs-tehr

pilot
**der Pilot** m /
**die Pilotin** f
dehr pee-LOHT /
dee pee-LOH-tihn

policeman
**der Polizist** m /
**die Polizistin** f
dehr poh-lee-TSIHST /
dee poh-lee-TSIHS-tihn

coach
**der Trainer** m /
**die Trainerin** f
dehr TREH-nehr /
dee TREH-neh-rihn

sailor
**der Matrose** m /
**die Matrosin** f
dehr maht-ROH-zuh /
dee maht-ROH-zihn

soldier
**der Soldat** m /
**die Soldatin** f
dehr zohl-DAHT /
dee zohl-DAH-tihn

teacher
**der Lehrer** m /
**die Lehrerin** f
dehr LEH-rehr /
dee LEH-reh-rihn

judge
**der Richter** m /
**die Richterin** f
dehr RIHSH-tehr /
dee RIHSH-teh-rihn

tailor
**der Schneider** m /
**die Schneiderin** f
dehr SHNIE-dehr /
dee SHNIE-deh-rihn

veterinarian
**der Tierarzt** m /
**die Tierärztin** f
dehr TEER-ahrtst /
dee TEER-ehrts-tihn

waiter
**der Kellner** m /
**die Kellnerin** f
dehr KEHL-nehr /
dee KEHL-neh-rihn

mechanic
**der Mechaniker** m /
**die Mechanikerin** f
dehr meh-SHAH-nee-kehr /
dee meh-SHAH-nee-keh-rihn

| engineer | **der Ingenieur _m_ / die Ingenieurin _f_** | dehr ihn-geh-NEEUHR / dee ihn-geh-NEEUH-rihn |
| craftsman | **der Handwerker _m_ / die Handewerkerin _f_** | dehr HANT-vehr-kehr / dee HANT-vehr-keh-rihn |
| dentist | **der Zahnarzt _m_ / die Zahnärztin _f_** | dehr TSAHN-ahrtst / dee TSAHN-ehrts-tihn |
| driver | **der Fahrer _m_ / die Fahrerin _f_** | dehr FAH-rehr / dee FAH-reh-rihn |
| barber | **der Friseur _m_ / die Friseuse _f_** | dehr free-ZER / dee free-ZER-zuh |
| beautician | **die Kosmetikerin** | dee kohs-MEH-tee-keh-rihn |
| broker | **der Broker _m_ / die Brokerin _f_** | dehr BROH-kehr / dee BROH-keh-rihn |
| accountant | **der Buchhalter _m_ / die Buchhalterin _f_** | dehr BOOKH-khahl-tehr / dee BOOKH-khahl-teh-rihn |
| pharmacist | **der Apotheker _m_ / die Apothekerin _f_** | dehr ah-poh-TEH-kehr / dee ah-poh-TEH-keh-rihn |
| writer | **der Schriftsteller _m_ / die Schriftstellerin _f_** | dehr SHRIHFT-shteh-lehr / dee SHRIHFT-shteh-leh-rihn |
| politician | **der Politiker _m_ / die Politikerin _f_** | dehr poh-LEE-tee-kehr / dee poh-LEE-tee-keh-rihn |
| professor | **der Professor _m_ / die Professorin _f_** | dehr proh-FEH-sohr / dee proh-feh-SOH-rihn |
| salesman | **der Verkäufer _m_ / die Verkäuferin _f_** | dehr vehr-KOY-fehr / dee vehr-KOY-feh-rihn |
| shoemaker | **der Schuhmacher _m_ / die Schuhmacherin _f_** | dehr SHOOH-mah-khehr / dee SHOOH-mah-kheh-rihn |
| watchmaker | **der Uhrmacher _m_ / die Uhrmacherin _f_** | dehr OOR-mah-khehr / dee OOR-mah-kheh-rihn |
| What's your occupation? | **Was bist du / sind Sie von Beruf?** | vahs bihst doo / zihnt zee fohn beh-ROOF? |
| I work as a secretary. | **Ich arbeite als Sekräterin.** | ihsh AHR-bie-tuh ahls zeh-kreh-TEH-rihn |
| I am a teacher. | **Ich bin Lehrer / Lehrerin von Beruf.** | ihsh bihn LEH-rehr / LEH-reh-rihn fohn beh-ROOF |

desk
**der Schreibtisch**
dehr SHRIEP-tihsh

office
**das Büro**
dahs bew-ROH

computer
**der Computer**
dehr kohm-POO-tehr

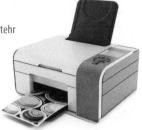

drawer
**die Schublade**
dee SHOOP-lah-
duh

printer
**der Drucker**
dehr DROO-kehr

filing cabinet
**der Aktenschrank**
dehr AHK-tehn-shrahnk

rubber stamp
**der Stempel**
dehr SHTEHM-pehl

telephone
**das Telefon**
dahs teh-leh-FOHN

ink pad
**das Stempelkissen**
dahs SHTEHM-pehl-kih-sehn

bin
**der Papierkorb**
dehr pah-PEER-kohrp

swivel chair
**der Drehstuhl**
dehr DRAY-shtool

keyboard
**die Tastatur**
dee tahs-tah-TOOR

| clipboard | **die Schreibunterlage** | dee SHRIEP-oon-tehr-lah-guh |
| file | **die Datei** | dee dah-TIE |
| in-tray | **die Ablage für Eingänge** | dee AHP-lah-guh fewr IEN-gehn-guh |
| to photocopy | **fotokopieren** | foh-toh-koh-PEE-rehn |
| to print | **drucken** | DROO-kehn |

bulldog clip
**die Papierklammer**
dee pah-PEER-klah-mehr

calculator
**der Taschenrechner**
dehr TAH-shehn-rehsh-nehr

correction tape
**das Korrekturband**
dahs koh-rehk-TOOR-bahnt

envelope
**der Umschlag**
dehr OOM-shlahk

laptop
**der Laptop**
dehr LEHP-tohp

highlighter
**der Markierstift**
dehr mahr-KEER-shtihft

letterhead
**das Firmenpapier**
dahs FIHR-mehn-pah-peer

holepunch
**der Locher**
dehr LOH-khehr

elastic bands
**die Gummibänder**
dee GOO-mee-behn-dehr

notepad
**der Notizblock**
dehr noh-TIHTS-blohk

pen
**der Kugelschreiber**
dehr KOO-gehl-shrie-behr

pencil sharpener
**der Spitzer**
dehr SHPIH-tsehr

paper clip
**die Büroklammer**
dee bew-ROH-klah-mehr

personal organiser
**der Terminplaner**
dehr tehr-MEEN-plah-nehr

pencil
**der Bleistift**
dehr BLIE-shtihft

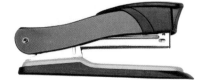

sticky tape
**der Tesafilm**
dehr TEH-zah-fihlm

stapler
**der Hefter**
dehr HEHF-tehr

staples
**die Heftklammern**
dee HEHFT-klah-mehrn

FOOD AND DRINK

apple juice
**der Apfelsaft**
dehr AHP-fehl-zahft

grapefruit juice
**der Grapefruitsaft**
dehr GREHP-froot-
zahft

orange juice
**der Orangensaft**
dehr oh-RAHN-gehn-
zahft

tomato juice
**der Tomatensaft**
dehr toh-MAH-tehn-sahft

coffee
**der Kaffee**
dehr KAH-feh

milk
**die Milch**
dee mihlsh

tea
**der Tee**
dehr teh

with lemon
**mit Zitrone**
miht tsee-TROH-nuh

water
**das Wasser**
dahs VAH-sehr

| with milk | **mit Milch** | miht mihlsh | decaffeinated | **entkoffeiniert** | ehnt-koh-feh-ee-NEERT |
| black | **schwarz** | shvahrts | fruit juice | **der Fruchtsaft** | dehr FROOKHT-zahft |

bacon
**der Bacon**
dehr BEH-kohn

banana
**die Banane**
dee bah-NAH-nuh

berries
**die Beeren**
dee BEH-rehn

biscuit
**der Keks**
dehr kehks

blueberries
**die Blaubeeren**
dee BLOW-beh-rehn

bread
**das Brot**
dahs broht

jam
**die Marmelade**
dee mahr-meh-LAH-duh

butter
**die Butter**
dee BOO-tehr

cereal
**die Frühstücksflocken**
dee FREW-shtewks-floh-kehn

cheese
**der Käse**
dehr KEH-zuh

cottage cheese
**der Frischkäse**
dehr FRIHSH-keh-zuh

doughnut
**der Donut**
dehr DOH-naht

egg
**das Ei**
dahs ie

ham
**der Schinken**
dehr SHIHN-kehn

honey
**der Honig**
dehr HOH-nihk

marmalade
**die Marmelade**
dee mahr-meh-LAH-duh

omelette
**das Omelett**
dahs ohm-LEHT

pancake
**der Pfannkuchen**
dehr PFAHN-koo-khehn

peanut butter
**die Erdnussbutter**
dee EHRT-noos-boo-tehr

sandwich
**der Sandwich**
dehr ZEHND-wihch

sausage
**die Wurst**
dee voorst

toast
**der Toast**
dehr tohst

waffle
**die Waffel**
dee VAH-fehl

yoghurt
**der Joghurt**
dehr YOH-goohrt

breakfast
**das Frühstück**
dahs FREW-shtewk

brunch
**der Brunch**
dehr brahnch

porridge
**der Haferbrei**
dehr HAH-fehr-brie

scrambled eggs
**das Rührei**
dahs REWR-ie

hard-boiled egg
**hart gekochtes Ei**
hahrt geh-KOHKH-tehs ie

soft-boiled egg
**weich gekochtes Ei**
viesh geh-KOHKH-tehs ie

| What do you eat for breakfast? | **Was isst du / essen Sie zum Frühstück?** | vahs ihst doo / EH-sehn zee tsoom FREW-shtewk? |
| When do you have breakfast? | **Wann frühstückst du / frühstücken Sie?** | vahn FREW-shtewkst doo / FREW-shtew-kehn zee? |
| When does breakfast start? | **Wann beginnt das Frühstück?** | vahn beh-GIHNT dahs FREW-shtewk? |
| What would you like to drink? | **Was möchtest du / möchten Sie trinken?** | vahs MERSH-tehst doo / MERSH-tehn zee TRIHN-kehn? |
| I would like a white tea. | **Ich möchte gern weißen Tee.** | ihsh MERSH-tuh gehrn VIE-sehn teh |

bacon
**der Bacon**
dehr BEH-kohn

beef
**das Rindfleisch**
dahs RIHNT-fliesh

chicken
**das Hähnchen**
dahs HEHN-shehn

duck
**die Ente**
dee EHN-tuh

ham
**der Schinken**
dehr SHIHN-kehn

kidneys
**die Nieren**
dee NEE-rehn

lamb
**das Lammfleisch**
dahs LAHM-fliesh

liver
**die Leber**
dee LEH-behr

mince
**das Hackfleisch**
dahs HAHK-fliesh

pâté
**die Pastete**
dee pahs-TEH-tuh

salami
**die Salami**
dee zah-LAH-mee

meat
**das Fleisch**
dahs fliesh

rabbit
**das Kaninchen**
dahs kah-NIHN-shehn

pork
**das Schweinefleisch**
dahs SHVIE-neh-fliesh

sausage
**die Wurst**
dee voorst

turkey
**der Puter**
dehr POO-tehr

veal
**das Kalbfleisch**
dahs KAHLP-fliesh

fruits
**das Obst**
dahs ohpst

apple
**der Apfel**
dehr AHP-fehl

apricot
**die Aprikose**
dee ah-pree-KOH-zuh

banana
**die Banane**
dee bah-NAH-nuh

blackberry
**die Brombeere**
dee BROHM-beh-ruh

blackcurrant
**schwarze Johannisbeere**
SHVAR-tsuh joh-HAH-nihs-beh-ruh

blueberry
**die Blaubeere**
dee BLOW-beh-ruh

cherry
**die Kirsche**
dee KIHR-shuh

coconut
**die Kokosnuss**
dee KOH-kohs-noos

fig
**die Feige**
dee FIE-guh

grape
**die Traube**
dee TROW-buh

grapefruit
**die Grapefruit**
dee GREHP-froot

kiwi fruit
**die Kiwi**
dee KEE-vee

lemon
**die Zitrone**
dee tsee-TROH-nuh

lime
**die Limette**
dee lee-MEH-tuh

mango
**die Mango**
dee MAHN-goh

melon
**die Melone**
dee meh-LOH-nuh

orange
**die Orange**
dee oh-RAHN-guh

peach
**der Pfirsich**
dehr PFIHR-zihsh

pear
**die Birne**
dee BIHR-nuh

lychee
**die Litschi**
dee lee-chee

clementine
**die Klementine**
dee kleh-mehn-TEE-nuh

papaya
**die Papaya**
dee pah-PAH-yah

pineapple
**die Ananas**
dee AH-nah-nahs

watermelon
**die Wassermelone**
dee VAH-sehr-meh-LOH-nuh

kumquat
**die Kumquat**
dee KOOM-kvaht

nectarine
**die Nektarine**
dee neh-ktah-REE-nuh

raspberry
**die Himbeere**
dee HIHM-beh-ruh

persimmon
**die Persimone**
dee pehr-zee-MOH-nuh

plum
**die Pflaume**
dee PFLOW-muh

redcurrant
**rote Johannisbeere**
ROH-tuh joh-HAH-nihs-beh-ruh

rhubarb
**der Rhabarber**
dehr rah-BAHR-behr

pomegranate
**der Granatapfel**
dehr grah-NAHT-ahp-fehl

strawberry
**die Erdbeere**
dee EHRT-beh-ruh

passion fruit
**die Passionsfrucht**
dee pah-SEEONS-frookht

vegetables
**das Gemüse**
dahs geh-MEW-zuh

artichoke
**die Artischocke**
dee ahr-tee-SHOH-kuh

asparagus
**der Spargel**
dehr SHPAHR-gehl

avocado
**die Avocado**
dee ah-voh-KAH-doh

beansprouts
**die Bohnensprossen**
dee BOH-nehn-shproh-sehn

beetroot
**rote Beete**
ROH-tuh BEE-tuh

broccoli
**der Brokkoli**
dehr BROH-koh-lee

Brussels sprouts
**der Rosenkohl**
dehr ROH-zehn-kohl

cabbage
**der Kohl**
dehr kohl

aubergine
**die Aubergine**
dee oh-behr-GEEN

carrot
**die Karotte**
dee kah-ROH-tuh

101

cauliflower
**der Blumenkohl**
dehr BLOO-mehn-kohl

celery
**die Sellerie**
dee ZEH-leh-ree

courgette
**die Zucchini**
dee tsoo-KEE-nee

cucumber
**die Gurke**
dee GOOR-kuh

garlic
**der Knoblauch**
dehr KNOHP-lowkh

ginger
**der Ingwer**
dehr IHN-gvehr

leek
**der Lauch**
dehr lowkh

lettuce
**grüner Zalat**
GREW-nehr sah-LAHT

mushroom
**der Pilz**
dehr pihlts

onion
**die Zwiebel**
dee TSVEE-behl

peas
**die Erbsen**
dee EHRP-sehn

potato
**die Kartoffel**
dee kahr-TOH-fehl

pumpkin
**der Kürbis**
dehr KEWR-bihs

sweetcorn
**der Mais**
dehr mays

spinach
**der Spinat**
dehr shpee-NAHT

tomato
**die Tomate**
dee toh-MAH-tuh

radish
**das Radieschen**
dahs rah-DEES-shen

spring onion
**die Frühlingszwiebel**
dee FREW-lihngs-zvee-behl

red pepper
**der Paprika**
dehr PAH-pree-kah

green beans
**grüne Bohnen**
GREW-nuh BOH-nehn

chicory
**der Chicorée**
dehr shee-koh-REH

turnip
**die Rübe**
dee REW-buh

cuttlefish
**der Tintenfisch**
dehr TIHN-tehn-fihsh

haddock
**der Schellfisch**
dehr SHEHL-fihsh

lemon sole
**die Rotzunge**
dee ROHT-tsoon-guh

halibut
**der Heilbutt**
dehr HIEL-boot

mackerel
**die Makrele**
dee mah-KREH-luh

monkfish
**der Seeteufel**
dehr ZEH-toy-fehl

mussels
**die Muscheln**
dee MOO-shehln

sardine
**die Sardine**
dee zahr-DEE-nuh

sea bass
**der Seebarsch**
dehr ZEH-bahrsh

sea bream
**die Dorade**
dee doh-RAH-duh

swordfish
**der Schwertfisch**
dehr SHVEHRT-fihsh

trout
**die Forelle**
dee foh-REH-luh

crab
**die Krabbe**
dee KRAH-buh

crayfish
**der Flusskrebs**
dehr FLOOS-krehps

lobster
**der Hummer**
dehr HOO-mehr

tuna
**der Thunfisch**
dehr TOON-fihsh

octopus
**der Krake**
dehr KRAH-kuh

oyster
**die Auster**
dee OWS-tehr

prawn / shrimp
**die Garnele**
dee gahr-NEH-luh

scallop
**die Jakobsmuschel**
dee YAH-kohps-moo-shehl

salmon
**der Lachs**
dehr lahks

squid
**der Kalmar**
dehr KAHL-mahr

| fish | **der Fisch** | dehr fihsh |
|---|---|---|
| cleaned | **gereinigt** | geh-RIE-nihkt |
| fresh | **frisch** | frihsh |
| frozen | **gefroren** | geh-FROH-rehn |
| salted | **gesalzen** | geh-ZAHL-tsehn |
| skinned | **gehäutet** | geh-HOY-teht |
| smoked | **geräuchert** | geh-ROY-shehrt |

cheese
**der Käse**
dehr KEH-zuh

cream
**die Sahne**
dee ZAH-nuh

egg
**das Ei**
dahs ie

milk
**die Milch**
dee mihlsh

cottage cheese
**der Frischkäse**
dehr FRIHSH-keh-zuh

blue cheese
**der Blauschim-
melkäse**
dehr BLOW-shih-me-
hl-keh-zuh

butter
**die Butter**
dee BOO-tehr

| | | | | | |
|---|---|---|---|---|---|
| goat's cheese | **der Ziegenkäse** | dehr TSEE-gehn-keh-zuh | semi-skimmed milk | **die Halbmagermilch** | dee HAHLP-mah-gehr-mihlsh |
| crème fraîche | **die Crème fraîche** | dee krehm-FREHSH | skimmed milk | **die Magermilch** | dee MAH-gehr-mihlsh |
| margarine | **die Margarine** | dee mahr-gah-REE-nuh | sour cream | **der Sauerrahm** | dehr ZO-wehr-rahm |
| full-fat milk | **die Vollmilch** | dee FOHL-mihlsh | yoghurt | **der Joghurt** | dehr YOH-goort |

baguette
**die Baguette**
dee bah-GEHT

bread roll
**das Brötchen**
dahs BRERT-shehn

brown bread
**das Vollkornbrot**
dahs FOHL-kohrn-broht

cake
**der Kuchen**
dehr KOO-khehn

loaf
**der Laib**
dehr liep

white bread
**das Weißbrot**
dahs VIES-broht

| quiche | **die Quiche** | dee keesh | pastry | **das Gebäck** | dahs geh-BEHK |
|---|---|---|---|---|---|
| sliced loaf | **in Scheiben geschnittenes Brot** | ihn SHIE-behn geh-SHNIH-teh-nehs broht | pitta bread | **das Pitabrot** | dahs PEE-tah-broht |
| garlic bread | **das Knoblauchbrot** | dahs KNOHP-lowkh-broht | sponge cake | **der Biskuitkuchen** | dehr BIHS-kveet-koo-khehn |

ketchup
**der Ketchup**
dehr KEH-choop

mayonnaise
**die Mayonnaise**
dee mah-yoh-NEH-zuh

mustard
**der Senf**
dehr zehnf

vinegar
**der Essig**
dehr EH-sihk

salt
**das Salz**
dahs zahlts

pepper
**der Pfeffer**
dehr PFEH-fehr

| | | |
|---|---|---|
| basil | **das Basilikum** | dahs bah-ZEE-lee-koom |
| chilli powder | **das Chilipulver** | dahs CHEE-lee-pool-fehr |
| chives | **der Schnittlauch** | dehr SHNIHT-lowkh |
| cinnamon | **der Zimt** | dehr tsihmt |
| coriander | **der Koriander** | dehr koh-ree-AHN-dehr |
| cumin | **der Kreuzkümmel** | dehr KROYTS-kew-mehl |
| curry | **der Curry** | dehr KEH-ree |
| dill | **der Dill** | dehr dihl |
| nutmeg | **die Muskatnuss** | dee moos-KAHT-noos |

| | | |
|---|---|---|
| paprika | **der Paprika** | dehr PAH-pree-kah |
| parsley | **die Petersilie** | dee peh-tehr-ZEE-leeuh |
| rosemary | **der Rosmarin** | dehr ROHZ-mah-rihn |
| saffron | **der Safran** | dehr ZAH-frahn |
| sage | **der Salbei** | dehr zahl-BIE |
| salad dressing | **die Salatsoße** | dee zah-LAHT-zoh-suh |
| spices | **die Gewürze** | dee geh-VEWR-tsuh |
| thyme | **der Thymian** | dehr TEW-mee-yan |
| vinaigrette | **die Vinaigrette** | dee vee-neh-GREHT |

bag
**die Tüte**
dee TEW-tuh

bar
**die Tafel**
dee TAH-fehl

bottle
**die Flasche**
dee FLAH-shuh

carton
**die Packung der Karton**
dee PAH-koonk dehr kahr-TOHN

jar
**das Glas**
dahs glahs

box
**die Box**
dee bohx

pack
**das Päckchen**
dahs PEHK-shehn

packet
**die Packung**
dee PAH-koonk

punnet
**das Körbchen /
die Schale**
dahs KERP-shehn /
dee SHAH-luh

| a bag of potatoes | **ein Sack Kartoffeln** | ien zahk kahr-TOH-fehln |
|---|---|---|
| chocolate bar | **eine Tafel Schokolade** | IE-nuh TAH-fehl shoh-koh-LAH-duh |
| two bottles of mineral water | **zwei Flaschen Mineralwasser** | tsvie FLAH-shehn mee-neh-RAHL-vah-sehr |
| a carton of milk | **eine Packung Milch** | IE-nuh PAH-koonk mihlsh |
| a jar of jam | **ein Glas Marmelade** | ien glahs mahr-meh-LAH-duh |

109

# 06

biscuit
**der Keks**
dehr kehks

chocolate bar
**die Schokoladentafel**
dee shoh-koh-LAH-dehn-tah-fehl

chocolate cake
**der Schokoladenkuchen**
dehr shoh-koh-LAH-dehn-koo-khehn

apple pie
**der Apfelkuchen**
dehr AHP-fehl-koo-khehn

doughnut
**der Donut**
dehr DOH-naht

fruit cake
**der Obstkuchen**
dehr OHPST-koo-khehn

fruit salad
**der Fruchtsalat**
dehr FROOKHT-Zah-laht

cheesecake
**der Käsekuchen**
dehr KEH-zuh-koo-khehn

gingerbread
**der Lebkuchen**
dehr LEHP-koo-khehn

ice cream
**das Eis**
dahs ies

muffin
**der Muffin**
dehr MAH-fihn

chocolate mousse
**die Schokoladenmousse**
dee shoh-koh-LAH-dehn-moos

milkshake
**der Milchshake**
dehr MIHLSH-shehyk

marshmallow
**das Marshmallow**
dahs MAHRSH-mah-low

macaroon
**die Makrone**
dee mah-KROH-nuh

waffle
**die Waffel**
dee VAH-fehl

pancakes
**der Pfannkuchen**
dehr PFAHN-koo-khehn

strudel
**der Strudel**
dehr SHTROO-dehl

pudding
**der Pudding**
dehr POO-dihnk

honey
**der Honig**
dehr HOH-nihk

| | | |
|---|---|---|
| cake | **der Kuchen** | dehr KOO-khehn |
| coconut cake | **der Kokosnusskuchen** | dehr KOH-kohs-noos-koo-khehn |
| dessert | **das Dessert** | dahs deh-SEHRT |
| frozen yoghurt | **gefrorener Joghurt** | geh-FROH-reh-nehr YOH-goort |
| rice pudding | **der Reispudding** | dehr RIES-poo-dihnk |
| I like to eat sweets. | **Ich esse gern Süßigkeiten.** | ihsh EH-suh gehrn SEW-sihsh-kie-tehntehn |
| I cannot eat anything sweet. | **Ich kann nichts Süßes essen.** | ihsh kahn nihshts SEW-sehs EH-sehn |

cheeseburger
**der Cheeseburger**
dehr CHEES-boor-gehr

hot dog
**der Hotdog**
dehr HOHT-dohk

fish sandwich
**der Fisch-Sandwich**
dehr FIHSH-zehnd-wihch

fried chicken
**gebratenes Hähnchen**
geh-BRAH-teh-nehs HEHN-shehn

French fries
**die Pommes frites**
dee pohm-FREETS

nachos
**die Nachos**
dee NAH-chohs

taco
**der Taco**
dehr TAH-koh

burrito
**der Burrito**
dehr boo-REE-toh

pizza
**die Pizza**
dee PIH-tsah

hamburger
**der Hamburger**
dehr HAHM-boor-gehr

chicken sandwich
**der Hühnchensandwich**
dehr HEHN-shehn-zehnd-wihch

fish and chips
**Fisch und Pommes**
fihsh oont POH-mehs

| | | |
|---|---|---|
| to peel | **schälen** | SHEH-lehn |
| to grate | **reiben** | RIE-behn |
| to chop | **hacken** | HAH-kehn |
| to crush | **zerkleinern** | tsehr-KLIE-nehrn |
| to beat | **schlagen** | SHLAH-gehn |
| to grease | **fetten** | FEH-tehn |
| to break | **brechen** | BREH-shehn |
| to stir | **rühren** | REW-rehn |
| to knead | **kneten** | KNEH-tehn |
| to steam | **dämpfen** | DEHMP-fehn |
| to weigh | **wiegen** | VEE-gehn |
| to add | **hinzufügen** | hihn-TSOO-few-gehn |
| to bake | **backen** | BAH-kehn |
| to stir-fry | **unter Rühren anbraten** | OON-tehr REW-rehn AHN-brah-tehn |
| to grill | **grillen** | GRIH-lehn |
| to roast | **rösten** | RERS-tehn |
| to barbecue | **braten** | BRAH-tehn |
| to fry | **in der Pfanne braten** | ihn dehr PFAH-nuh BRAH-tehn |

to wash
**waschen**
VAH-shehn

to cut
**schneiden**
SHNIE-dehn

to mix
**mischen**
MIH-shehn

to boil
**kochen**
KOH-hkehn

bar
**die Bar**
dee bahr

buffet
**das Büfett**
dahs bew-FEH

bill
**die Rechnung**
dee REHSH-noonk

bistro
**das Bistro**
dahs BIHS-troh

café
**das Café**
dahs kah-FEH

dessert
**die Nachspeise**
dee NAHKH-shpie-zuh

menu
**die Speisekarte**
dee SHPIE-zeh-kahr-tuh

canteen
**die Kantine**
dee kahn-TEE-nuh

pizzeria
**die Pizzeria**
dee pih-tseh-REE-yah

pub
**die Kneipe**
dee KNIE-puh

salad bar
**die Salatbar**
dee zah-LAHT-bahr

deli
**die Delikatessen**
dee deh-lee-kah-TEH-sehn

self-service
**die Selbstbedienung**
dee ZEHLPST-beh-dee-noonk

take-out / take-away
**zum Mitnehmen**
tsoom MIHT-nehy-mehn

waiter
**der Kellner**
dehr KEHL-nehr

waitress
**die Kellnerin**
dee KEHL-neh-rihn

| | | |
|---|---|---|
| à la carte | **à la carte** | ah-lah-KART |
| starter | **der Appetizer** | dehr ah-peh-TIE-zehr |
| booking | **die Reservierung** | dee reh-zehr-VEE-roonk |
| complimentary | **gratis** | GRAH-tihs |
| dish | **das Gericht** | dahs geh-RIHSHT |
| main course | **das Hauptgericht** | dahs HOWPST-geh-ri-hkht |
| to order | **bestellen** | beh-SHTEH-lehn |
| speciality | **die Spezialität** | dee shpeh-tsee-ah-lee-TEHT |
| aperitif | **der Aperitif** | dehr ah-peh-ree-TEEF |

| | | |
|---|---|---|
| What do you want to order? | **Was willst du / wollen Sie bestellen?** | vahs vihlst doo / VOH-lehn zee beh-SHTEH-lehn? |
| I would like to see the menu. | **Ich hätte gern die Speisekarte.** | ihsh HEH-tuh gehrn dee SHPIE-zeh-kahr-tuh |
| We'll take the set menu. | **Wir nehmen das Menü.** | veer NEHY-mehn dahs meh-NEW |

# TRAVEL AND LEISURE

to travel by bus
**mit dem Bus reisen**
miht dehm boos RIE-zehn

to travel by plane
**mit dem Flugzeug reisen**
miht dehm FLOOK-tsoyk RIE-zehn

to travel by car
**mit dem Auto reisen**
miht dehm OW-toh RIE-zehn

to travel by bicycle
**mit dem Fahrrad reisen**
miht dehm FAH-raht RIE-zehn

to travel by motorcycle
**mit dem Motorrad reisen**
miht dehm MOH-toh-raht RIE-zehn

travel agency
**das Reisebüro**
dahs RIE-zuh-bew-roh

family holiday
**der Familienurlaub**
dehr fah-MEE-leeuhn-oor-lowp

safari
**die Safari**
dee zah-FAH-ree

beach holiday
**der Strandurlaub**
dehr SHTRAHNT-oor-lowp

honeymoon
**die Flitterwochen**
dee FLIH-tehr-voh-khehn

round-the-world trip
**die Weltreise**
dee VEHLT-rie-zuh

cruise
**die Kreuzfahrt**
dee KROYTS-fahrt

to book
**buchen**
BOO-hkehn

long-haul destination
**fernes Ziel**
FEHR-nehs tseehl

guided tour
**die Führung**
dee FEW-roonk

out of season
**außerhalb der Saison**
OW-sehr-hahlp dehr zeh-ZOHN

picturesque village
**das malerische Dorf**
dahs mah-LEH-ree-shuh dohrf

landscape
**die Landschaft**
dee LANT-shahft

to go sightseeing
**besichtigen**
beh-ZIHSH-tee-gehn

city break
**die Städtereise**
dee SHTEH-tuh-rie-zuh

| | | |
|---|---|---|
| holiday brochure | **die Urlaubsbroschüre** | dee OOR-lowps-broh-shew-ruh |
| holiday destination | **das Reiseziel** | dahs RIE-zuh-tseehl |
| package tour | **die Pauschalreise** | dee pow-SHAHL-rie-zuh |
| places of interest | **die Sehenswürdigkeiten** | dee ZEH-yehns-vewr-dihsh-kie-tehn |
| short break | **der Kurzurlaub** | dehr KOORTS-oor-lowp |
| tourist attractions | **touristische Attraktionen** | too-RIHS-tee-shuh ah-trahk-TSEEOH-nehn |
| tourist trap | **die Touristenfalle** | dee too-RIHS-tehn-fah-luh |

Afghanistan
**Afghanistan**
ahf-GAH-nihs-tahn

Albania
**Albanien**
ahl-BAH-neeuhn

Algeria
**Algerien**
ahl-GEH-reeuhn

Andorra
**Andorra**
ahn-DOH-rah

Angola
**Angola**
ahn-GOH-lah

Antigua and Barbuda
**Antigua und Barbuda**
ahn-TEE-kwah unt
bahr-BOO-dahh

Argentina
**Argentinien**
ahr-gehn-TEE-neeuhn

Armenia
**Armenien**
ahr-MEH-neeuhn

Aruba
**Aruba**
ah-ROO-bah

Australia
**Australien**
ows-TRAH-leeuhn

Austria
**Österreich**
ERS-teh-riekh

Azerbaijan
**Aserbaidschan**
ah-zehr-bie-DCHAHN

The Bahamas
**Bahamas**
bah-HAH-mahs

Bahrain
**Bahrain**
bah-RIEN

Bangladesh
**Bangladesch**
bahn-glah-DEHSH

Barbados
**Barbados**
bahr-BAH-dohs

Belarus
**Weißrussland**
VIES-roos-lant

Belgium
**Belgien**
BEHL-geeuhn

Belize
**Belize**
beh-LEES

Benin
**Benin**
beh-NEEN

Bhutan
**Bhutan**
BOO-tahn

Brazil
**Brasilien**
brah-ZEE-leeuhn

Burma
**Birma**
BIHR-mah

Canada
**Kanada**
KAH-nah-dah

Chile
**Chile**
CHEE-luh

Bolivia
**Bolivien**
boh-LEE-veeuhn

Brunei
**Brunei**
BROO-nay

Burundi
**Burundi**
boo-ROON-dee

Cape Verde
**Kap Verde**
kahp VEHR-duh

China
**China**
SHEE-nah

Bosnia and Herzegovina
**Bosnien und Herzegowina**
BOHS-neeuhn unt hehr-
tseh-GOH-vee-nah

Bulgaria
**Bulgarien**
bool-GAH-reeuhn

Cambodia
**Kambodscha**
kahm-BOH-dchah

Central African Republic
**Zentralafrikanische Republik**
tsehn-TRAHL-ah-free-kah-nee-
shuh reh-poo-BLEEK

Colombia
**Kolumbien**
koh-LOOM-beeuhn

Botswana
**Botswana**
bots-VAH-nah

Burkina Faso
**Burkina Faso**
boor-KEE-nah FAH-soh

Cameroon
**Kamerun**
KAH-meh-roon

Chad
**Tschad**
chaht

Comoros
**Komoren**
koh-MOH-rehn

121

Democratic Republic
of the Congo
**Demokratische
Republik Kongo**
deh-moh-KRAH-tee-shuh
reh-poo-BLEEK KOHN-goh

Republic of the Congo
**Republik Kongo**
reh-poo-BLEEK KOHN-goh

Costa Rica
**Costa Rica**
KOHS-tah REE-kah

Côte d'Ivoire
**Elfenbeinküste**
EHL-fehn-bien-kews-tuh

Croatia
**Kroatien**
kroh-AH-teeuhn

Cuba
**Kuba**
KOO-bah

Curacao
**Curacao**
kew-rah-SAH-oh

Cyprus
**Zypern**
TSEW-pehrn

Czechia
**Tschechien**
CHEH-sheeuhn

Denmark
**Dänemark**
DEH-neh-mahrk

Djibouti
**Dschibuti**
dchee-BOO-tee

Dominica
**Dominica**
doh-MEE-nee-kah

Dominican Republic
**Dominikanische Republik**
doh-mee-nee-KAH-nee-shuh
reh-poo-BLEEK

East Timor
**Osttimor**
ohst-TEE-mohr

Ecuador
**Ecuador**
eh-kwah-DOHR

Egypt
**Ägypten**
eh-GEWP-tehn

El Salvador
**El Salvador**
ehl zahl-vah-DOHR

Equatorial Guinea
**Äquatorialguinea**
eh-kvah-toh-ree-YAHL-
gee-neh-ah

Eritrea
**Eritrea**
eh-ree-TREH-ah

Estonia
**Estland**
EHST-lahnt

France
**Frankreich**
FRAHNK-riesh

Germany
**Deutschland**
DOYCH-lahnt

Guatemala
**Guatemala**
gwah-teh-MAH-lah

Haiti
**Haiti**
hah-EE-tee

Ethiopia
**Äthiopien**
eh-TEEOH-peeuhn

Gabon
**Gabun**
gah-BOON

Ghana
**Ghana**
GAH-nah

Guinea
**Guinea**
gee-NEH-ah

Honduras
**Honduras**
hohn-DOO-rahs

Fiji
**Fidschi**
FEE-dchee

The Gambia
**Gambia**
GAHM-bee-yah

Greece
**Griechenland**
GREE-shehn-lahnt

Guinea-Bissau
**Guinea-Bissau**
gee-NEH-ah-BEE-sow

Hong Kong
**Hongkong**
HOHNK-kohnk

Finland
**Finnland**
FIHN-lahnt

Georgia
**Georgien**
geh-OHR-geeuhn

Grenada
**Grenada**
greh-NAH-dah

Guyana
**Guyana**
goo-YAH-nah

Hungary
**Ungarn**
OON-gahrn

Iceland
**Island**
EES-lant

Iraq
**Irak**
ee-RAHK

Jamaica
**Jamaika**
yah-MAHY-kah

Kenya
**Kenia**
KEH-nee-yah

Kosovo
**Kosovo**
KOH-soh-voh

India
**Indien**
IHN-deeuhn

Ireland
**Irland**
IHR-lahnt

Japan
**Japan**
YAH-pahn

Kiribati
**Kiribati**
kee-ree-BAH-tee

Kuwait
**Kuwait**
koo-VIET

Indonesia
**Indonesien**
ihn-doh-NEH-zeeuhn

Israel
**Israel**
IHS-rah-ehl

Jordan
**Jordanien**
yohr-DAH-neeuhn

North Korea
**Nordkorea**
nort-koh-REH-ah

Kyrgyzstan
**Kirgisistan**
kihr-GEE-zee-stahn

Iran
**Iran**
ee-RAHN

Italy
**Italien**
ee-TAH-leeuhn

Kazakhstan
**Kasachstan**
kah-zahkh-STAHN

South Korea
**Südkorea**
zewt-koh-REH-ah

Laos
**Laos**
LAH-ohs

Latvia
**Lettland**
LEHT-lahnt

Libya
**Libyen**
LEE-beeuhn

Macau
**Macau**
mah-KAU

Malaysia
**Malaysia**
mah-LEH-zee-yah

Marshall Islands
**Marshallinseln**
MAHR-shahl-ihn-zehln

Lebanon
**Libanon**
LEE-bah-nohn

Liechtenstein
**Liechtenstein**
LEEKH-tehn-shtien

Macedonia
**Mazedonien**
mah-tseh-DOH-neeuhn

Maldives
**Malediven**
mah-leh-DEE-vehn

Mauritania
**Mauretanien**
mow-reh-TAH-neeuhn

Lesotho
**Lesotho**
leh-SOH-toh

Lithuania
**Litauen**
LEE-to-wehn

Madagascar
**Madagaskar**
mah-dah-GAHS-kahr

Mali
**Mali**
MAH-lee

Mauritius
**Mauritius**
mow-REE-tee-oos

Liberia
**Liberia**
lee-BEH-ree-yah

Luxembourg
**Luxemburg**
LOO-xehm-boork

Malawi
**Malawi**
mah-LAH-vee

Malta
**Malta**
MAHL-tah

Mexico
**Mexiko**
MEH-xee-koh

Micronesia
**Mikronesien**
mee-kroh-NEH-zeeuhn

Montenegro
**Montenegro**
mohn-teh-NEH-groh

Nauru
**Nauru**
nah-OO-roo

Nicaragua
**Nicaragua**
nee-kah-RAH-goo-ah

Oman
**Oman**
oh-MAHN

Moldova
**Moldawien**
mohl-DAH-veeuhn

Morocco
**Marokko**
mah-ROH-koh

Nepal
**Nepal**
NEH-pahl

Niger
**Niger**
NEE-gehr

Pakistan
**Pakistán**
pah-kees-TAHN

Monaco
**Monaco**
moh-NAH-koh

Mozambique
**Mosambik**
moh-zahm-BEEK

Netherlands
**Niederlande**
NEE-dehr-lahn-duh

Nigeria
**Nigeria**
nee-GEH-ree-yah

Palau
**Palau**
PAH-low

Mongolia
**Mongolei**
mohn-goh-LIE

Namibia
**Namibia**
nah-MEE-bee-yah

New Zealand
**Neuseeland**
noy-ZEH-lahnt

Norway
**Norwegen**
nohr-VEH-gehn

Palestinian Territories
**Palästinensische Gebiete**
pah-lehs-tee-NEHN-zih-shuh geh-BEE-tuh

Panama
**Panama**
PAH-nah-mah

Philippines
**Philippinen**
fee-lee-PEE-nehn

Romania
**Rumänien**
roo-MEH-neeuhn

Samoa
**Samoa**
zah-MOH-ah

Serbia
**Serbien**
ZEHR-beeuhn

Papua New Guinea
**Papua-Neuguinea**
pah-poo-ah-noy-gee-NEH-ah

Poland
**Polen**
POH-lehn

Russia
**Russland**
ROOS-lahnt

San Marino
**San Marino**
zahn mah-REE-noh

Seychelles
**Seychellen**
zeh-SHEH-lehn

Paraguay
**Paraguay**
PAH-rah-gwuay

Portugal
**Portugal**
POHR-too-gahl

Rwanda
**Ruanda**
roo-AHN-dah

Saudi Arabia
**Saudi Arabien**
ZOW-dee ah-RAH-beeuhn

Sierra Leone
**Sierra Leone**
SEEEHR-rah leh-OH-nuh

Peru
**Peru**
peh-ROO

Qatar
**Katar**
KAH-tahr

Saint Lucia
**Saint Lucia**
sihnt LOO-see-yah

Senegal
**Senegal**
ZEH-neh-gahl

Singapore
**Singapur**
SEEHN-gah-poor

Sint Maarten
**Sint Maarten**
sihnt MAH-ahr-tehn

Somalia
**Somalia**
zoh-MAH-lee-yah

Sudan
**Sudan**
zoo-DAHN

Sweden
**Schweden**
SHVEH-dehn

Tajikistan
**Tadschikistan**
tah-DCHEE-kihs-tahn

Slovakia
**Slowakei**
sloh-vah-KIE

South Africa
**Südafrika**
zewt-AH-free-kah

South Sudan
**Südsudan**
ZEWT-zoo-dahn

Switzerland
**Schweiz**
shviets

Tanzania
**Tansania**
tahn-zah-NEE-yah

Slovenia
**Slowenien**
sloh-VEH-neeuhn

Spain
**Spanien**
SHPAH-neeuhn

Suriname
**Surinam**
zoo-ree-NAHM

Syria
**Syrien**
ZEW-reeuhn

Thailand
**Thailand**
TIE-lahnt

Solomon Islands
**Salomonen**
zah-loh-MOH-nehn

Sri Lanka
**Sri Lanka**
sree LAHN-kah

Swaziland
**Swasiland**
SVAH-zee-lahnt

Taiwan
**Taiwan**
tie-VAHN

Togo
**Togo**
TOH-goh

Tonga
**Tonga**
TOHN-gah

Turkmenistan
**Turkmenistan**
toork-MEH-nihs-tahn

United Arab Emirates
**Vereinigte Arabische
Emirate**
vehr-IE-nihk-tuh ah-RAH-
bih-shuh eh-mee-RAH-tuh

Uruguay
**Uruguay**
oo-roo-GWUAY

Vietnam
**Vietnam**
vee-eht-NAHM

Trinidad and Tobago
**Trinidad und Tobago**
TREE-nee-daht oont
toh-BAH-goh

Tuvalu
**Tuvalu**
too-VAH-loo

United Kingdom
**Vereinigtes Königreich**
veh-IE-nihk-tehs KEW-nih-
kh-riesh

Uzbekistan
**Usbekistan**
oos-BEH-kihs-tahn

Yemen
**Jemen**
YEH-mehn

Tunisia
**Tunesien**
too-NEH-zeeuhn

Uganda
**Uganda**
oo-GAHN-dah

United States of America
**Vereinigte Staaten
von Amerika**
vehr-IE-nihk-tuh SHTAH-tuh
fohn ah-MEH-ree-kah

Vanuatu
**Vanuatu**
veh-noo-AH-too

Zambia
**Sambia**
ZAHM-bee-yah

Turkey
**Türkei**
tewr-KIE

Ukraine
**Ukraine**
oo-krah-EE-nuh

Venezuela
**Venezuela**
veh-neh-zoo-EH-lah

Zimbabwe
**Simbabwe**
zeem-BAHB-wuh

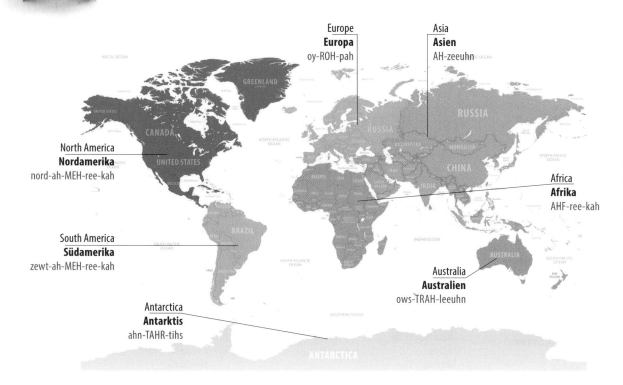

Europe
**Europa**
oy-ROH-pah

Asia
**Asien**
AH-zeeuhn

North America
**Nordamerika**
nord-ah-MEH-ree-kah

Africa
**Afrika**
AHF-ree-kah

South America
**Südamerika**
zewt-ah-MEH-ree-kah

Australia
**Australien**
ows-TRAH-leeuhn

Antarctica
**Antarktis**
ahn-TAHR-tihs

bus stop
**die Haltestelle**
dee HAHL-teh-steh-luh

platform
**der Bahnsteig**
dehr BAHN-shtiek

(aero)plane
**das Flugzeug**
dahs FLOOK-tsoyk

moped / scooter
**das Moped**
dahs MOH-peht

(bi)cycle
**das Fahrrad**
dahs FAH-raht

boat
**das Boot**
dahs boht

bus
**der Bus**
dehr boos

ship
**das Schiff**
dahs shihf

car
**das Auto**
dahs OW-toh

helicopter
**der Hubschrauber**
dehr HOOP-shrow-behr

lorry
**der LKW**
dehr ehl-kah-VEH

tanker
**der Tanker**
dehr TAHN-kehr

kids' scooter
**der Roller**
dehr ROH-lehr

(motor)bike
**das Motorrad**
dahs MOH-toh-raht

train
**der Zug**
dehr tsook

taxi
**das Taxi**
dahs TAH-xih

ferry
**die Fähre**
dee FEH-ruh

submarine
**das U-Boot**
dahs OO-boot

sailing boat
**das Segelboot**
dahs ZEH-gehl-boht

tram
**die Straßenbahn**
dee SHTRAH-sehn-bahn

| by air | **mit dem Flugzeug** | miht dehm FLOOK-tsoyk |
| on the motorway | **auf der Autobahn** | owf dehr OW-toh-bahn |
| on the road | **auf der Straße** | owf dehr SHTRAH-suh |
| by sea | **auf dem Seeweg** | owf dehm ZEH-vehk |

airport
**der Flughafen**
dehr FLOOK-hah-fehn

arrivals
**die Ankünfte**
dee AHN-kewnf-tuh

departures
**die Abflüge**
dee AHP-flew-guh

luggage
**das Gepäck**
dahs geh-PEHK

carry-on luggage
**das Handgepäck**
dahs HAHNT-geh-pehk

oversized baggage
**übergroßes Gepäck**
EW-behr-groh-sehs geh-PEHK

check-in desk
**der Abfertigungsschalter**
dehr AHP-fehr-tee-goonks-shahl-tehr

customs
**der Zoll**
dehr tsohl

baggage reclaim
**die Gepäckausgabe**
dee geh-PEHK-ows-gah-buh

boarding pass
**die Bordkarte**
dee BOHRT-kahr-tuh

flight ticket
**das Flugticket**
dahs FLOOK-tih-keht

economy class
**die Economyklasse**
dee ihh-KOH-noh-mih-klah-suh

business class
**die Businessklasse**
dee bihs-nuhs-KLAH-suh

arrivals lounge
**die Ankunftslounge**
dee AHN-koonfts-lowng

delayed
**verspätet**
fehr-SHPEH-teht

to board a plane
**ins Flugzeug einsteigen**
ihns FLOOK-tsoyk IEN-shtie-gehn

gate
**der Flugsteig**
dehr FLOOK-stiek

passport
**der Pass**
dehr pahs

passport control
**die Passkontrolle**
dee PAHS-kohn-troh-luh

security check
**die Sicherheitskontrolle**
dee ZIH-shehr-khiets-kohn-troh-luh

| airline | **die Fluggesellschaft** | dee FLOOK-geh-zehl-shahft | return ticket | **das Rückflugticket** | dahs REWK-flook-tih-keht |
|---|---|---|---|---|---|
| boarding time | **die Einsteigezeit** | dee IEN-stie-guh-tsiet | one-way ticket | **das einfache Ticket** | dahs IEN-fah-khuh TIH-keht |
| charter flight | **der Charterflug** | dehr CHAHR-tehr-flook | The flight has been delayed. | **Der Flug hat sich verzögert.** | dehr flook haht zihsh fehr-zer-gehrt |
| long-haul flight | **der Langstreckenflug** | dehr LAHNK-shtreh-kehn-flook | to book a ticket to … | **ein Ticket nach … buchen** | ien TIH-keht nakh … boo-khehn |
| on time | **pünktlich** | PEWNKT-lihsh | | | |

railway station
**der Bahnhof**
dehr BAHN-hohf

train
**der Zug**
dehr tsook

platform
**der Bahnsteig**
dehr BAHN-shtiek

| express train | **der Express-Zug** | dehr ehx-PREHS-tsook |
| to get on the train | **in den Zug einsteigen** | ihn dehn tsook IEN-shtie-gehn |
| to get off the train | **aus dem Zug aussteigen** | ows dehm tsook OWS-shtie-gehn |
| to miss a train | **einen Zug verpassen** | IE-nehn tsook vehr-PAH-sehn |

train driver
**der Zugführer**
dehr TSOOK-few-rehr

travelcard
**die Netzfahrkarte**
dee NEHTS-fahr-kahr-tuh

train journey
**die Zugreise**
dee TSOOK-rie-zuh

carriage
**der Wagen**
dehr VAH-gehn

seat
**der Sitzplatz**
dehr ZIHTS-plahts

station
**die Station**
dee shtah-TSEEOHN

restaurant car
**der Speisewagen**
dehr SHPIE-zuh-vah-gehn

sleeper train
**der Schlafzug**
dehr SHLAHF-tsook

toilet
**die Toilette**
dee too-ah-LEH-tuh

coach
**der Bus**
dehr boos

bus driver
**der Busfahrer**
dehr BOOS-fah-rehr

bus stop
**die Bushaltestelle**
dee BOOS-hahl-tuh-shteh-luh

validator
**der Entwerter**
dehr ENT-vehr-tehr

double-decker bus
**der Doppeldecker-Bus**
dehr DOH-pehl-deh-kehr-boos

bus journey
**die Busfahrt**
dee BOOS-fahrt

coach station
**der Busbahnhof**
dehr BOOS-bahn-hohf

request stop
**die Bedarfshaltestelle**
dee beh-DAHRFS-hahl-teh-shteh-luh

| | | |
|---|---|---|
| bus fare | **der Busfahrpreis** | dehr BOOS-fahr-pries |
| the next stop | **die nächste Haltestelle** | dee NEHKH-stuh HAHL-teh-shteh-luh |
| night bus | **der Nachtbus** | dehr NAHKHT-boos |
| to get on the bus | **in den Bus einsteigen** | ihn dehn boos IEN-shtie-gehn |
| to get off the bus | **aus dem Bus aussteigen** | ows dehm boos OWS-shtie-gehn |
| to miss a bus | **einen Bus verpassen** | IE-nehn boos fehr-PAH-sehn |

hotel
**das Hotel**
dahs hoh-TEHL

campsite
**das Camping**
dahs KEHM-pihnk

holiday resort
**der Urlaubsort**
dehr OOR-lowps-ohrt

youth hostel
**die Jugendherberge**
dee YOO-gehnt-heh-behr-guh

| | | |
|---|---|---|
| accommodation | **die Unterkunft** | dee OON-tehr-koonft |
| all-inclusive | **all-inclusive** | ohl-ihn-KLOO-sihf |
| half-board | **die Halbpension** | dee HAHLP-pahn-zeeohn |
| full-board | **die Vollpension** | dee FOHL-pahn-zeeohn |
| self-catering | **die Selbstversorgung** | dee ZEHLPST-vehr-zohr-goonk |
| I'm looking for a place to stay. | **Ich suche eine Unterkunft.** | ihsh ZOO-khuh IE-nuh OON-tehr-koonft |
| Can you recommend a hotel? | **Wo kann man dort übernachten?** | voo kahn mahn dohrt ew-behr-NAHKH-tehn? |
| We are staying at the hotel "XZ". | **Wir bleiben im Hotel „XZ".** | veer BLIE-behn ihm hoh-TEHL „XZ" |
| Have you already booked the hotel? | **Hast du / Haben Sie das Hotel schon gebucht?** | hahst doo / HAH-behn zee dahs hoh-TEHL shohn geh-BOOKHT? |

bed and breakfast
**Übernachtung mit Frühstück**
ew-behr-NAHKH-toonk miht
FREW-shtewk

single bed
**das Einzelbett**
dahs IEN-tsehl-beht

double bed
**das Doppelbett**
dahs DOH-pehl-beht

floor
**die Etage**
dee eh-TAH-guh

front desk / reception
**die Rezeption**
dee reh-tsehp-TSEEOHN

hotel manager
**die Hotelmanagerin** *f*
dee hoh-TEHL-meh-nah-geh-rihn

indoor pool
**der Innenpool**
dehr IHNEHN-pool

key
**der Schlüssel**
dehr SHLEW-sehl

kitchenette
**die Kochnische**
dee KOHKH-nee-shuh

luggage cart
**der Gepäckwagen**
dehr geh-PEHK-vah-gehn

towels
**die Handtücher**
dee HAHNT-tew-shehr

room service
**der Zimmerservice**
dehr TSIH-mehr-sehr-vihs

lobby
**die Lobby**
dee loh-bee

wake-up call
**der Weckruf**
dehr VEHK-roof

reservation
**die Reservierung**
dee reh-zehr-VEE-roonk

guest
**der Gast**
dehr gahst

| check-in | **das Check-in** | dahs chehk-IHN |
| check-out | **das Check-out** | dahs chehk-OWT |
| complimentary breakfast | **kostenloses Frühstück** | KOHS-tehn-loh-zehs FREWH-shtewk |
| king-size bed | **das Kingsize-Bett** | dahs KIHNK-siez-beht |
| late charge | **der Verspätungszuschlag** | dehr vehr-SHPEH-toonks-tsoo-shlahk |
| full | **voll belegt** | fohl beh-LEHKT |
| parking pass | **die Parkkarte** | dee PAHRK-kahr-tuh |
| pay-per-view movie | **der Pay-per-View-Film** | dehr pehy-pehr-VEEYOO-fihlm |
| queen-size bed | **das Queensize-Bett** | dahs KWEEN-siez-beht |
| rate | **der Tarif** | dehr tah-REEF |
| vacancy | **freie Zimmer** | FRAH-yuh TSIH-mehr |

city-centre / downtown
**die Innenstadt**
dee IHNEHN-shtaht

capital
**die Hauptstadt**
dee HOWPT-shtaht

centre
**das Zentrum**
dahs TSEHN-troom

district
**der Bezirk**
dehr beh-TSIHRK

industrial zone
**das Industrieviertel**
dahs ihn-doos-TREE-feer-tehl

city
**die Stadt**
dee shtaht

metropolis
**die Metropole**
dee meh-troh-POH-luh

region
**die Region**
dee reh-GEEOHN

seaside resort
**der Badeort**
dehr BAH-duh-ohrt

old town
**die Altstadt**
dee AHLT-shtaht

ski resort
**der Skiort**
dehr SKEE-ohrt

small town
**die Kleinstadt**
dee KLIEN-shtaht

suburb
**der Vorort**
dehr FOHR-ohrt

village
**das Dorf**
dahs dohrf

winter resort
**der Wintersportort**
dehr VIHN-tehr-shpohrt-ohrt

alley
**der Parkweg**
dehr pahrk-vehk

boulevard
**der Boulevard**
dehr boo-leh-VAHR

motorway
**die Autobahn**
dee OW-toh-bahn

country road
**die Landstraße**
dee LAHNT-shtrah-suh

toll road
**die Mautstraße**
dee MOWT-shtrah-suh

street
**die Straße**
dee SHTRAH-suh

bicycle lane
**der Radweg**
dehr RAHT-vehk

bicycle path
**der Fahrradweg**
dehr FAH-raht-vehk

crossroads / intersection
**die Kreuzung**
dee KROY-tsoonk

traffic lights
**die Ampel**
dee AHM-pehl

red light
**das Rotlicht**
dahs ROHT-lihsht

orange light
**das Gelblicht**
dahs GEHLP-lihsht

green light
**das Grünlicht**
dahs GREWN-lihsht

roundabout
**der Kreisverkehr**
dehr KRIES-fehr-kehr

pedestrian crossing
**der Fußgängerüberweg**
dehr FOOS-gehn-gehr-ew-behr-vehk

pavement
**der Bürgersteig**
dehr BEWR-gehr-shtiek

bridge
**die Brücke**
dee BREW-kuh

footbridge
**der Brückenübergang**
dehr BREW-kehn-ew-behr-gahnk

overpass
**die Überführung**
dee EW-behr-few-roonk

underpass
**die Unterführung**
dee OON-tehr-few-roonk

tunnel
**der Tunnel**
dehr TOO-nehl

road
**der Weg**
dehr vehk

street corner
**die Straßenecke**
dee SHTRAH-sehn-eh-kuh

one-way street
**die Einbahnstraße**
dee IEN-bahn-shtrah-suh

| | | |
|---|---|---|
| avenue | **die Allee** | dee ah-LEHEH |
| expressway | **die Schnellstraße** | dee SHNEHL-shtrah-suh |
| four-lane road | **eine vierspurige Straße** | IE-nuh FEER-shpoo-ree-guh SHTRAH-suh |
| main road | **die Hauptstraße** | dee HOWPT-shtrah-suh |
| side street | **die Nebenstraße** | dee NEH-behn-shtrah-suh |
| two-lane road | **eine zweispurige Straße** | IE-nuh TSVIE-shpoo-ree-guh SHTRAH-suh |
| fast lane | **die Überholspur** | dee ew-behr-HOHL-shpoor |
| left lane | **die linke Spur** | dee LIHN-kuh shpoor |
| right lane | **die rechte Spur** | dee REHKH-tuh shpoor |
| breakdown lane | **die Pannenspur** | dee PAH-nehn shpoor |

attractions
**die Sehenswürdigkeiten**
dee ZEH-yehns-vewr-dihsh-kie-tehn

casino
**das Kasino**
dahs kah-ZEE-noh

guide book
**der Reiseführer**
dehr RIE-zuh-few-rehr

park
**der Park**
dehr pahrk

guided tour
**der Reiseführer**
dehr RIE-zuh-few-rehr

information
**die Information**
dee ihn-fohr-mah-TSEEOHN

itinerary
**die Reiseroute**
dee RIE-zuh-roo-tuh

ruins
**die Ruinen**
dee roo-EE-nehn

monument
**das Monument**
dahs moh-noo-MEHNT

museum
**das Museum**
dahs moo-ZEH-oom

national park
**der Nationalpark**
dehr nah-tseeoh-NAHL-pahrk

sightseeing
**die Besichtigung**
dee beh-ZIHSH-tee-goonk

souvenirs
**die Andenken**
dee AHN-dehn-kehn

tour bus
**der Tourbus**
dehr TOOR-boos

tourist
**der Tourist *m* / die Touristin *f***
dehr too-RIHST / dee too-RIHS-tihn

| entrance fee / price | **der Eintrittspreis** | dehr IEN-trihts-pries |
| to buy a souvenir | **ein Souvenir kaufen** | ien zoo-veh-NEER KOW-fehn |
| to do a tour | **eine Tour machen** | EI-nuh toor MAH-khehn |
| tour guide | **der Reiseführer** | dehr RIE-zuh-few-rehr |

airport
**der Flughafen**
dehr FLOOK-hah-fehn

bank
**die Bank**
dee bahnk

bus stop
**die Bushaltestelle**
dee BOOS-hahl-tuh-shteh-luh

church
**die Kirche**
dee KIHR-shuh

cinema
**das Kino**
dahs KEE-noh

city / town hall
**das Rathaus**
dahs RAHT-hows

department store
**das Kaufhaus**
dahs KOWF-hows

factory
**die Fabrik**
dee fah-BREEK

fire station
**die Feuerwehr**
dee FO-yehr-vehr

hospital
**das Krankenhaus**
dahs KRAHN-kehn-hows

hotel
**das Hotel**
dahs hoh-TEHL

library
**die Bibliothek**
dee bee-bleeoh-TEHK

theatre
**das Theater**
dahs teh-AH-tehr

museum
**das Museum**
dahs moo-ZEH-oom

parking area
**der Parkplatz**
dehr PAHRK-plahts

playground
**der Spielplatz**
dehr SHPEEL-plahts

police station
**die Polizei**
dee poh-lee-TSIE

post office
**die Post**
dee pohst

prison
**das Gefängnis**
dahs geh-FEHNK-nihs

restaurant
**das Restaurant**
dahs rehs-toh-RAHN

school
**die Schule**
dee SHOO-luh

taxi stand
**der Taxistand**
dehr TAH-xee-shtahnt

harbour
**der Hafen**
dehr HAH-fehn

square
**der Platz**
dehr plahts

supermarket
**der Supermarkt**
dehr ZOO-pehr-mahrkt

railway station
**der Bahnhof**
dehr BAHN-hohf

| How do I get to the railway station? | **Wie komme ich zum Bahnhof?** | vee KOH-muh ihsh tsoom BAHN-hohf? |
| Where can I find a taxi? | **Wo finde ich ein Taxi?** | voh FIHN-duh ihsh ien TAH-xee? |

snorkel
**der Schnorchel**
dehr SHNOHR-shehl

diving mask
**die Tauchmaske**
dee TOWKH-mahs-kuh

swimming goggles
**die Schwimmbrille**
dee SHVIHM-brih-luh

beach ball
**der Wasserball**
dehr VAH-sehr-bahl

hat
**der Hut**
dehr hoot

sunglasses
**die Sonnenbrille**
dee ZOH-nehn-brih-luh

sunscreen
**das Sonnenschutzmittel**
dahs ZOH-nehn-shoots-mih-tehl

beach towel
**das Badetuch**
dahs BAH-duh-tookh

beach
**der Strand**
dehr shtrahnt

sun lounger
**der Liegestuhl**
dehr LEE-guh-shtool

| swimming cap | **die Schwimmhaube** | dee SHVIHM-how-buh |
| bikini | **der Bikini** | dehr bee-KEE-nee |
| swimming costume | **der Badeanzug** | dehr BAH-duh-ahn-tsook |
| to sunbathe | **sich sonnen** | zihsh ZOH-nehn |
| to swim | **schwimmen** | SHVIH-mehn |

 HEALTH

medicines
**die Medikamente**
dee meh-dee-kah-MEHN-tuh

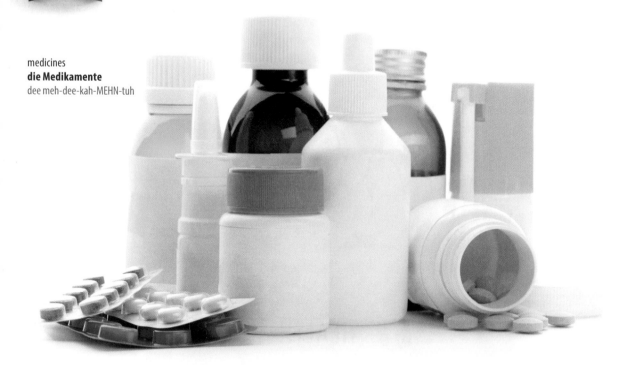

eye drops
**die Augentropfen**
dee OW-gehn-trohp-fehn

painkiller
**das Schmerzmittel**
dahs SHMEHRTS-mih-tehl

syrup
**der Sirup**
dehr ZEE-roop

to take medicine
**ein Medikament einnehmen**
ien meh-dee-kah-MEHNT
IE-neh-mehn

shot / injection
**die Injektion**
dee ihn-yehk-TSEEON

sleeping pill
**die Schlaftablette**
dee SHLAHF-tah-bleh-tuh

plaster
**der Pflaster**
dehr PFLAHS-tehr

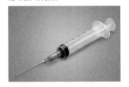

syringe
**die Spritze**
dee SHPRIH-tsuh

gauze
**die Gaze**
dee GAH-zuh

pill
**die Pille**
dee PIH-luh

tablet
**die Tablette**
dee tah-BLEH-tuh

ointment
**die Salbe**
dee ZAHL-buh

hospital
**das Krankenhaus**
dahs KRAHN-kehn-hows

nurse
**der Krankenpfleger** *m* **/ die Krankenschwester** *f*
dehr KRAHN-kehn-pfleh-gehr /
dee KRAHN-kehn-shvehs-tehr

doctor / physician
**der Arzt** *m* **/ die Ärztin** *f*
dehr ahrtst / dee EHRTS-tihn

operation / surgery
**die Operation**
dee oh-peh-rah-TSEEOHN

patient
**der Patient** *m* **/ die Patientin** *f*
dehr pah-TSEEUHNT / dee pah-TSEEUHN-tihn

waiting room
**das Wartezimmer**
dahs VAHR-tuh-tsih-mehr

| | | | | | |
|---|---|---|---|---|---|
| check-up | **die Untersuchung** | dee oon-tehr-ZOO-hoonk | prescription | **das Rezept** | dahs reh-TSEHPT |
| diagnosis | **die Diagnose** | dee deeahg-NOH-zuh | specialist | **der Spezialist** | dehr shpeh-tseeah-LIHST |
| pharmacy / chemist's | **die Apotheke** | dee ah-poh-TEH-kuh | treatment | **die Behandlung** | dee beh-HAHND-loonk |

allergist
**der Allergologe** *m* **/ die Allergologin** *f*
dehr ah-lehr-goh-LOH-guh /
 dee ah-lehr-goh-LOH-gihn

dentist
**der Zahnarzt** *m* **/ die Zahärztin** *f*
dehr TSAHN-ahrtst /
dee TSAHN-ehrts-tihn

gynecologist
**der Frauenarzt** *m* **/ die Frauenärztin** *f*
dehr FROW-ehn-ahrtst /
dee FROW-ehn-ehrts-tihn

pediatrician
**der Kinderarzt** *m* **/ die Kinderärztin** *f*
dehr KIHN-dehr-ahrtst /
dee KIHN-dehr-ehrts-tihn

physiotherapist
**der Physiotherapeut** *m* **/**
**die Physiotherapeutin** *f*
dehr FEW-zeeoh-teh-rah-poyt /
dee FEW-zeeoh-teh-rah-poy-tihn

midwife
**die Hebamme** *f*
dee HEH-bah-muh

ophthalmologist
**der Augenarzt** *m* **/ die Augenärztin** *f*
dehr OW-gehn-ahrtst /
dee OW-gehn-ehrts-tihn

surgeon
**der Chirurg** *m* **/ die Chirurgin** *f*
dehr shee-ROORK /
dee shee-ROOR-gihn

| | | |
|---|---|---|
| anaesthesiologist | **der Anästhesist** *m* **/ die Anästhesistin** *f* | dehr ah-nehs-teh-ZIHST / dee ah-nehs-teh-ZIHS-tihn |
| cardiologist | **der Kardiologe** *m* **/ die Kardiologin** *f* | dehr kahr-deeoh-LOH-guh / dee kahr-deeoh-LOH-gihn |
| dermatologist | **der Dermatologe** *m* **/ die Dermatologin** *f* | dehr dehr-mah-toh-LOH-guh / dee dehr-mah-toh-LOH-gihn |
| neurologist | **der Neurologe** *m* **/ die Neurologin** *f* | dehr noy-roh-LOH-guh / dee noy-roh-LOH-gihn |
| oncologist | **der Onkologe** *m* **/ die Onkologin** *f* | dehr ohn-koh-loh-guh / dee ohn-koh-loh-gihn |
| psychiatrist | **der Psychiater** *m* **/ die Psychiaterin** *f* | dehr psew-sheeah-tuhr / dee psew-sheeah-teh-rihn |
| radiologist | **der Radiologe** *m* **/ die Radiologin** *f* | dehr rah-deeoh-loh-guh / dee rah-deeoh-loh-gihn |

to feel good
**sich gut fühlen**
zihsh goot FEW-lehn

to catch a cold
**sich erkälten**
zihsh ehr-KEHL-tehn

to have a cold
**erkältet sein**
ehr-KEHL-teht zien

to sneeze
**niesen**
NEE-zehn

to cough
**husten**
HOOS-tehn

to blow one's nose
**sich die Nase putzen**
zihsh dee NAH-zuh POO-tsehn

to feel sick
**sich krank fühlen**
zihsh krahnk FEW-lehn

to faint
**in Ohnmacht fallen**
ihn OHN-mahkht FAH-lehn

to pass out
**bewusstlos werden**
beh-VOOST-lohs VEHR-dehn

to be tired
**müde sein**
MEW-duh zien

to be exhausted
**erschöpft sein**
ehr-SHERPFT zien

to have back pain
**Rückenschmerzen haben**
REW-kehn-shmehr-tsehn HAH-behn

to have earache
**Ohrenschmerzen haben**
OH-rehn-shmehr-tsehn HAH-behn

to have a headache
**Kopfschmerzen haben**
KOHPF-shmehr-tsehn hah-behn

to have a sore throat
**Halsschmerzen haben**
HAHLS-shmehr-tsehn HAH-behn

to have toothache
**Zahnschmerzen haben**
TSAHN-shmehr-tsehn HAH-behn

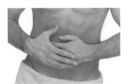
to have a stomach ache
**Magenschmerzen haben**
MAH-gehn-shmehr-tsehn HAH-behn

to have a temperature
**Fieber haben**
FEE-behr HAH-behn

to have diarrhoea
**Durchfall haben**
DOORSH-fahl HAH-behn

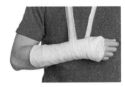
to break an arm
**den Arm brechen**
dehn ahrm BREH-shehn

to have constipation
**Verstopfung haben**
fehr-SHTOHP-foonk HAH-behn

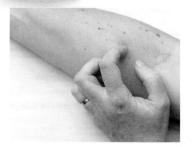

to have a rash
**einen Ausschlag haben**
EI-nehn OWS-shlahk HAH-behn

to be allergic to
**allergisch sein gegen**
ah-LEHR-gihsh zien geh-gehn

to vomit
**sich übergeben**
zihsh ew-behr-GEH-behn

to hurt
**sich verletzen**
zihsh fehr-LEH-tsehn

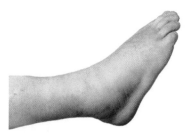

to swell
**anschwellen**
AHN-shveh-lehn

to suffer from
**an etwas leiden**
ahn EHT-fahs LIE-dehn

chicken pox
**die Windpocken**
dee VIHNT-poh-kehn

runny nose
**der Schnupfen**
dehr SHNOOP-fehn

heart attack
**der Herzinfarkt**
dehr HEHRTS-ihn-fahrkt

cough
**der Husten**
dehr HOOS-tehn

diarrhoea
**der Durchfall**
dehr DOORSH-fahl

fever
**das Fieber**
dahs FEE-behr

headache
**die Kopfschmerzen**
dee kohpf-shmehr-tsehn

injury
**die Verletzung**
dee fehr-LEH-tsoonk

sore throat
**die Halsschmerzen**
dee HAHLS-shmehr-tsehn

asthma
**das Asthma**
dahs AHST-mah

flu
**die Grippe**
dee GRIH-puh

health
**die Gesundheit**
dee geh-ZOONT-hiet

hepatitis
**die Hepatitis**
dee heh-pah-TEE-tihs

heart disease
**die Herzkrankheit**
dee HEHRTS-krahnk-hiet

stomach ache
**die Bauchschmerzen**
dee BOWKH-shmehr-tsehn

mouth ulcer
**das Mundgeschwür**
dahs MOOHNT-geh-shwewr

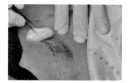

wound
**die Wunde**
dee VOON-duh

| | | | | | |
|---|---|---|---|---|---|
| common cold | **die Erkältung** | dee ehr-KEHL-toonk | pain | **der Schmerz** | dehr shmehrts |
| fracture | **der Bruch** | dehr brookh | painful | **schmerzlich** | SHMEHRTS-lihsh |
| illness | **die Krankheit** | dee KRAHNK-hiet | painless | **schmerzlos** | SHMEHRTS-lohs |
| mumps | **der Mumps** | dehr moomps | to be ill | **krank sein** | krahnk zien |

emergency number
**die Notrufnummer**
dee NOHT-roof-noo-mehr

firefighter
**der Feuerwehrmann**
dehr FO-yehr-vehr-mahn

policeman
**der Polizist**
dehr poh-lee-TSIHST

fire engine
**der Feuerwehrwagen**
dehr FO-yehr-vah-gehn

police car
**das Polizeiauto**
dahs poh-lee-TSIE-ow-toh

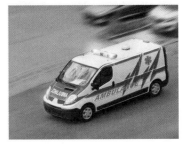

ambulance
**der Rettungswagen**
dehr REH-toonks-vah-gehn

accident
**der Unfall**
dehr OON-fahl

paramedics
**die Sanitäter**
dee zah-nee-TEH-tehr

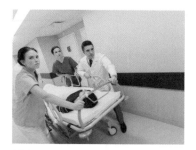

emergency
**die Notaufnahme**
dee NOHT-owf-nah-muh

fire
**das Feuer**
dahs FO-yehr

patient
**der Patient** *m* **/ die Patientin** *f*
dehr pah-TSEEUHNT / dee pah-TSEEUHN-tihn

police
**die Polizei**
dee poh-lee-TSIE

SPORT

badminton racket
**der Badmintonschläger**
dehr BEHT-mihn-tohn-shleh-
gehr

bowling ball
**die Bowlingkugel**
dee BOW-leenk-koo-gehl

net
**das Netz**
dahs nehts

ball
**der Ball**
dehr bahl

cap
**die Cap**
dee kehp

goggles
**die Schutzbrille**
dee SHOOTS-brih-luh

baseball
**der Baseball**
dehr BEHYS-bahl

football
**der Fußball**
dehr FOOS-bahl

golf ball
**der Golfball**
dehr GOHLF-bahl

bicycle
**das Fahrrad**
dahs FAH-raht

glove
**der Handschuh**
dehr HAHNT-shoo

helmet
**der Helm**
dehr hehlm

hockey puck
**die Eishockeyscheibe**
dee IES-hoh-kee-shie-buh

hockey stick
**der Hockeyschläger**
dehr HOH-kee-shleh-gehr

goal
**das Tor**
dahs tohr

saddle
**der Sattel**
dehr ZAH-tehl

ice-skates
**die Schlittschuhe**
dee SHLIHT-shoo-uh

lane
**die Bahn**
dee bahn

skates
**die Inlineskater**
dee IHN-lien-skey-tehr

ski poles
**die Skistöcke**
dee SHEE-shter-kuh

skis
**die Skier**
dee sheer

snowboard
**das Snowboard**
dahs SNOW-bohrt

surfboard
**das Surfbrett**
dahs SEHRF-breht

squash racket
**der Squashschläger**
dehr SKVOSH-shleh-gehr

swimming costume
**der Badeanzug**
dehr BAH-duh-ahn-tsook

tennis ball
**der Tennisball**
dehr TEH-nihs-bahl

tennis racket
**der Tennisschläger**
dehr TEH-nihs-shleh-gehr

volleyball
**der Volleyball**
dehr VOH-lehy-bahl

weights
**die Gewichte**
dee geh-VIHKH-tuh

baseball
**der Baseball**
dehr BEYS-bohl

bowling
**das Bowling**
dahs BOW-lihnk

football
**der Fußball**
dehr FOOS-bahl

hiking
**das Wandern**
dahs VAHN-dehrn

hockey
**das Eishockey**
dahs IES-hoh-kee

running
**das Laufen**
dahs LOW-fehn

cycling
**das Radfahren**
dahs RAHT-fah-rehn

horseriding
**das Reiten**
dahs RIE-tehn

skating
**das Skaten**
dahs SKEY-tehn

skiing
**das Skifahren**
dahs SHEE-fah-rehn

swimming
**das Schwimmen**
dahs SHVIH-mehn

tennis
**das Tennis**
dahs TEH-nihs

volleyball
**der Volleyball**
dehr VOH-ley-bahl

weightlifting
**das Gewichtheben**
dahs geh-VIHST-heh-behn

basketball court
**der Basketballspielplatz**
dehr BAHS-keht-bahl-shpeel-plahts

boxing ring
**der Boxring**
dehr BOHX-rihnk

golf course
**der Golfplatz**
dehr GOHLF-plahts

fitness centre
**das Fitnesscenter**
dahs FIHT-nehs-tsehn-tehr

football pitch
**das Fußballfeld**
dahs FOOS-bahl-fehlt

football ground
**der Fußballplatz**
dehr FOOS-bahl-plahts

golf club
**der Golfclub**
dehr GOHLF-kloop

gym
**das Fitnessstudio**
dahs FIHT-nehs-shtoo-deeoh

playground
**der Spielplatz**
dehr SHPEEL-plahts

racecourse
**die Pferderennbahn**
dee PFEHR-duh-rehn-bahn

race track
**die Rennstrecke**
dee rehn-shtreh-kuh

recreation area
**das Erholungsgebiet**
dahs ehr-HOH-loonks-geh-beet

skating rink
**die Eisbahn**
dee IES-bahn

sports ground
**der Sportplatz**
dehr SHPOHRT-plahts

stadium
**das Stadion**
dahs shtah-DEEOHN

swimming pool
**das Schwimmbad**
dahs SHVIHM-baht

tennis club
**der Tennisclub**
dehr TEH-nihs-kloop

tennis court
**der Tennisplatz**
dehr TEH-nihs-plahts

NATURE

landscape
**die Landschaft**
dee LAHNT-shahft

bay
**die Bucht**
dee bookht

beach
**der Strand**
dehr shtrahnt

cave
**die Höhle**
dee HER-luh

stream
**der Bach**
dehr bahkh

desert
**die Wüste**
dee VEWS-tuh

forest / woods
**der Wald**
dehr vahlt

hill
**der Hügel**
dehr HEW-gehl

earth
**die Erde**
dee EHR-duh

island
**die Insel**
dee IHN-zehl

lake
**der See**
dehr zeh

mountain
**der Berg**
dehr behrk

ocean
**der Ozean**
dehr OH-tseh-ahn

peak
**der Gipfel**
dehr GIHP-fehl

plain
**das Flachland**
dahs FLAHKH-lahnt

pond
**der Teich**
dehr tiesh

river
**der Fluss**
dehr floos

sea
**das Meer**
dahs mehr

brook
**der Strom**
dehr shtrohm

swamp
**der Sumpf**
dehr zoompf

valley
**das Tal**
dahs tahl

waterfall
**der Wasserfall**
dehr VAH-sehr-fahl

weather
**das Wetter**
dahs VEH-tehr

| What's the weather like? | **Wie ist das Wetter?** | vee ihst dahs VEH-tehr? |
| What's the forecast for tomorrow? | **Wie wird das Wetter morgen sein?** | vee vihrt dahs VEH-tehr MOHR-gehn zien? |

blizzard
**der Schneesturm**
dehr SHNEH-shtoorm

cold
**kalt**
kahlt

drizzle
**der Nieselregen**
dehr NEE-zehl-reh-gehn

flood
**die Flut**
dee floot

frost
**der Frost**
dehr frohst

humidity
**die Feuchtigkeit**
dee FOYSH-tihsh-kiet

Celsius
**das Celsius**
dahs TSEHL-seeoos

cyclone
**der Zyklon**
dehr tsew-KLOHN

dry
**trocken**
TROH-kehn

fog
**der Nebel**
dehr NEH-behl

hail
**der Hagel**
dehr HAH-gehl

hurricane
**der Hurrikan**
dehr hoo-ree-KAHN

cloud
**die Wolke**
dee VOHL-kuh

degree
**der Grad**
dehr graht

dry season
**die Trockenzeit**
dee TROH-kehn-tsiet

forecast
**die Wettervorhersage**
dee VEH-tehr-fohr-hehr-zah-guh

heat
**die Hitze**
dee HIH-tsuh

ice
**das Eis**
dahs ies

cloudy
**bewölkt**
beh-VERLKT

dew
**der Tau**
dehr tow

Fahrenheit
**das Fahrenheit**
dahs FAH-rehn-hiet

freeze
**einfrieren**
IEN-free-rehn

hot
**heiß**
hies

lightning
**der Blitz**
dehr blihts

rain
**der Regen**
dehr REH-gehn

rainy season
**die Regenzeit**
dee REH-gehn-tsiet

snowy
**schneebedeckt**
SHNEH-beh-dehkt

temperature
**die Temperatur**
dee tehm-peh-rah-TOOR

tsunami
**der Tsunami**
dehr TSOO-nah-mee

rainstorm
**der Regensturm**
dehr REH-gehn-shtoorm

sleet
**der Schneeregen**
dehr SHNEH-reh-gehn

storm
**der Sturm**
dehr shtoorm

thunder
**der Donner**
dehr DOH-nehr

typhoon
**der Taifun**
dehr tie-FOON

windy
**windig**
VIHN-dihk

rainbow
**der Regenbogen**
dehr REH-gehn-boh-gehn

snow
**der Schnee**
dehr shneh

sun
**die Sonne**
dee SOH-nuh

thunderstorm
**das Gewitter**
dahs geh-VIH-tehr

warm
**warm**
vahrm

rainy
**regnerisch**
REHK-neh-rihsh

snowstorm
**der Schneesturm**
dehr SHNEH-shtoorm

sunny
**sonnig**
ZOH-nihk

tornado
**der Tornado**
dehr tohr-NAH-doh

wind
**der Wind**
dehr vihnt

pet owner
**der Haustierbesitzer**
dehr HOWS-teer-beh-zih-tsehr

pet shop
**die Tierhandlung**
dee TEER-hahnt-loong

aquarium
**das Aquarium**
dahs ah-KVAH-ree-oom

cage
**der Käfig**
dehr KEH-fihk

canary
**der Kanarienvogel**
dehr kah-nah-REEUHN-foh-gehl

bird
**der Vogel**
dehr FOH-gehl

dog
**der Hund**
dehr HOONT

fish
**der Fisch**
dehr FIHSH

cat
**die Katze**
dee KAH-tsuh

gecko
**der Gecko**
dehr GEH-koh

hamster
**der Hamster**
dehr HAHM-stehr

guinea pig
**das Meerschweinchen**
dahs MEHR-shvien-shehn

lizard
**die Eidechse**
dee IE-dehk-suh

rat
**die Ratte**
dee RAH-tuh

mouse
**die Maus**
dee mows

rabbit
**das Kaninchen**
dahs kah-NIHN-shehn

parrot
**der Papagei**
dehr pah-pah-GIE

snake
**die Schlange**
dee SHLAHN-guh

spider
**die Spinne**
dee SHPIH-nuh

cow
**die Kuh**
dee koo

chicken
**das Huhn**
dahs hoon

donkey
**der Esel**
dehr EH-zehl

goose
**die Gans**
dee gahns

goat
**die Ziege**
dee TSEE-guh

horse
**das Pferd**
dahs pfehrt

sheep
**das Schaf**
dahs shahf

duck
**die Ente**
dee EHN-tuh

rabbit
**das Kaninchen**
dahs kah-NIHN-shehn

pig
**das Schwein**
dahs shvien

turkey
**der Truthahn**
dehr TROOT-hahn

giraffe
**die Giraffe**
dee GEE-rah-fuh

elephant
**der Elefant**
dehr eh-leh-FAHNT

jaguar
**der Jaguar**
dehr YAH-goo-ahr

tiger
**der Tiger**
dehr TEE-gehr

lion
**der Löwe**
dehr LER-vuh

leopard
**der Leopard**
dehr leh-oh-PAHRT

puma
**der Puma**
dehr POO-mah

hippopotamus
**das Nilpferd**
dahs NEEL-pfehrt

monkey
**der Affe**
dehr AH-fuh

chimpanzee
**der Schimpanse**
dehr shihm-PAHN-zuh

ostrich
**der Strauß**
dehr shtrows

sloth
**das Faultier**
dahs FOWL-teer

rhinoceros
**das Nashorn**
dahs NAHS-hohrn

armadillo
**das Gürteltier**
dahs GEWR-tehl-teer

iguana
**der Leguan**
dehr leh-goo-AHN

kangaroo
**das Känguru**
dahs KEHN-goo-roo

bear
**der Bär**
dehr behr

zebra
**das Zebra**
dahs TSEH-brah

hyena
**die Hyäne**
dee hew-EH-nuh

seal
**die Robbe**
dee ROH-buh

gazelle
**die Gazelle**
dee gah-TSEH-luh

antelope
**die Antilope**
dee ahn-tee-LOH-puh

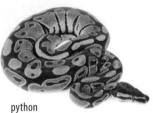

python
**der Python**
dehr PEW-tohn

water buffalo
**der Wasserbüffel**
dehr VAH-sehr-bew-fehl

boar
**das Wildschwein**
dahs VIHLT-shvien

cobra
**die Kobra**
dee KOH-brah

whale
**der Wal**
dehr vahl

killer whale
**der Killerwal**
dehr KIH-lehr-vahl

shark
**der Hai**
dehr hie

turtle
**die Schildkröte**
dee SHIHLT-krer-tuh

dolphin
**der Delfin**
dehr dehl-FEEN

crocodile
**das Krokodil**
dahs kroh-koh-DEEL

# SHOPPING AND SERVICES

grocery store
**das Lebensmittelgeschäft**
dahs LEH-behns-mih-tehl-geh-shehft

bazaar
**der Basar**
dehr bah-ZAHR

bookshop
**die Buchhandlung**
dee BOOKH-hahnt-loonk

computer shop
**das Computergeschäft**
dahs kohm-POO-tehr-geh-shehft

corner shop
**der Tante-Emma-Laden**
dehr tahn-tuh-EH-mah-lah-dehn

farmers' market
**der Bauernmarkt**
dehr BO-wehrn-mahrkt

flea market
**der Flohmarkt**
dehr FLOH-mahrkt

flower market
**der Blumenmarkt**
dehr BLOO-mehn-mahrkt

bakery
**die Bäckerei**
dee beh-keh-RIE

fruit stall
**der Obststand**
dehr OHPST-shtahnt

market
**der Markt**
dehr mahrkt

newsagent
**der Zeitungsstand**
dehr TSIE-toonks-shtahnt

shoe shop
**der Schuhladen**
dehr SHOO-lah-dehn

street vendor
**der Straßenverkäufer**
dehr SHTRAH-sehn-fehr-koy-fehr

supermarket
**der Supermarkt**
dehr ZOO-pehr-mahrkt

| department store | **das Kaufhaus** | dahs KOWF-hows |
| shopping centre | **das Einkaufszentrum** | dahs IEN-kowfs-tsehn-troom |

sale
**der Ausverkauf**
dehr OWS-fehr-kowf

checkout / till checkout
**die Kasse**
dee KAH-suh

conveyor belt
**das Förderband**
dahs FERR-dehr-bahnt

customer
**der Kunde *m* / die Kundin *f***
dehr KOON-duh / dee KOON-dihn

price
**der Preis**
dehr pries

queue
**die Warteschlange**
dee VAHR-tuh-shlahn-guh

receipt
**der Kassenbon**
dehr KAH-sehn-bohn

cashier
**der Kassierer *m* / die Kassiererin *f***
dehr kah-see-rehr / dee kah-see-reh-rihn

shopping bag
**die Einkaufstasche**
dee IEN-kowfs-tah-shuh

shopping list
**die Einkaufsliste**
dee IEN-kowfs-lihs-tuh

shopping basket
**der Einkaufskorb**
dehr IEN-kowfs-kohrp

trolley
**der Einkaufswagen**
dehr IEN-kowfs-vah-gehn

| | | |
|---|---|---|
| bill for | **die Rechnung für** | dee REHSH-noonk fewr |
| Can I help you? | **Kann ich Ihnen helfen?** | kahn ihsh EE-nehn HEHL-fehn? |
| goods | **die Waren** | dee VAH-rehn |
| shopper | **der Käufer** *m* / **die Käuferin** *f* | dehr koy-fehr / dee koy-feh-rihn |
| to cost | **kosten** | KOHS-tehn |
| to get a great bargain | **ein tolles Schnäppchen bekommen** | ien TOH-lehs SHNEHP-shehn beh-KOH-mehn |
| to purchase | **kaufen** | KOW-fehn |
| to queue | **Schlange stehen** | SHLAHN-guh SHTEH-yehn |

belt
**der Gürtel**
dehr GEWR-tehl

boots
**die Stiefel**
dee SHTEE-fehl

coat
**der Mantel**
dehr MAHN-tehl

raincoat
**der Regenmantel**
dehr REH-gehn-
mahn-tehl

gloves
**die Handschuhe**
dee HAHNT-shoo-uh

hat
**der Hut**
dehr hoot

jeans
**die Jeans**
dee geens

pyjamas
**der Pyjama**
dehr pew-GAH-mah

jacket
**die Jacke**
dee YAH-kuh

shoes
**die Schuhe**
dee SHOO-uh

jumper
**der Pullover**
dehr poo-LOH-vehr

scarf
**der Schal**
dehr shahl

underwear
**die Unterwäsche**
dee OON-tehr-veh-shuh

tie
**die Krawatte**
dee krah-VAH-tuh

briefs
**der Slip**
dehr slihp

shirt
**das Hemd**
dahs hehmt

sweatshirt
**das Sweatshirt**
dahs SVEHT-shihrt

suit
**der Anzug**
dehr AHN-tsook

t-shirt
**das T-Shirt**
dahs TEE-shihrt

trousers
**die Hose**
dee HOH-zuh

undershirt
**das Unterhemd**
dahs OON-tehr-hehmt

socks
**die Socken**
dee ZOH-kehn

slippers
**die Pantoffeln**
dee pahn-TOH-fehln

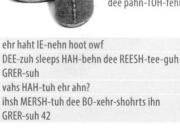

| He has a hat on. | **Er hat einen Hut auf.** | ehr haht IE-nehn hoot owf |
|---|---|---|
| These briefs are the right size. | **Diese Slips haben die richtige Größe.** | DEE-zuh sleeps HAH-behn dee REESH-tee-guh GRER-suh |
| What did he have on? | **Was hatte er an?** | vahs HAH-tuh ehr ahn? |
| I want these boxer shorts in a size 42. | **Ich möchte die Boxershorts in Größe 42.** | ihsh MERSH-tuh dee BO-xehr-shohrts ihn GRER-suh 42 |

jacket
**die Jacke**
dee YAH-kuh

jeans
**die Jeans**
dee geens

boots
**die Stiefel**
dee SHTEE-fehl

gloves
**die Handschuhe**
dee HAHNT-shoo-uh

hat
**der Hut**
dehr hoot

pyjamas
**der Pyjama**
dehr pew-GAH-mah

raincoat
**der Regenmantel**
dehr REH-gehn-mahn-tehl

belt
**der Gürtel**
dehr GEWR-tehl

coat
**der Mantel**
dehr MAHN-tehl

jumper
**der Pullover**
dehr poo-LOH-vehr

pants
**der Slip**
dehr slihp

scarf
**der Schal**
dehr shahl

skirt
**der Rock**
dehr rohk

dress
**das Kleid**
dahs kliet

shoes
**die Schuhe**
dee SHOO-uh

sweatshirt
**das Sweatshirt**
dahs SVEHT-shirt

socks
**die Socken**
dee ZOH-kehn

shirt
**das Hemd**
dahs hehmt

stockings
**die Strümpfe**
dee SHTREWMP-fuh

suit
**der Anzug**
dehr AHN-tsook

t-shirt
**das T-Shirt**
dahs TEE-shihrt

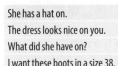

underwear
**die Unterwäsche**
dee OON-tehr-veh-shuh

slacks
**die Hose**
dee HOH-zuh

trousers
**die Hose**
dee HOH-zuh

slippers
**die Pantoffeln**
dee pahn-TOH-fehln

bra
**der Büstenhalter**
dehr BEW-stehn-hahl-tehr

| She has a hat on. | **Sie hat einen Hut auf.** | zee haht IE-nehn hoot owf |
|---|---|---|
| The dress looks nice on you. | **Das Kleid steht dir gut.** | dahs kliet shtehyt deer goot |
| What did she have on? | **Was hatte sie an?** | vahs HAH-tuh zee ahn? |
| I want these boots in a size 38. | **Ich möchte die Stiefel in Größe 38.** | ihsh MERSH-tuh dee SHTEE-fehl ihn GREW-suh 38 |

barber shop
**der Friseursalon**
dehr free-ZEWR-zah-lohn

beauty salon
**der Schönheitssalon**
dehr SHERN-hiets-zah-lohn

car repair shop
**die Kfz-Werkstatt**
dee kah-ehf-TSEH-vehrk-shtaht

bicycle repair shop
**die Fahrradwerkstatt**
dee FAH-raht-vehrk-shtaht

watchmaker
**die Uhrmacher-Werkstatt**
dee UHR-mah-khehr vehrk-shtaht

laundromat
**der Waschsalon**
dehr VAHSH-zah-lohn

dry cleaners
**die Wäscherei / die Reinigung**
dee veh-sheh-RIE /
dee RIE-nee-goonk

locksmiths
**der Schlüsseldienst**
dehr SHLEW-sehl-deenst

petrol station
**die Tankstelle**
dee TAHNK-shteh-luh

# CULTURE AND MEDIA

blog
**das Blog**
dahs blohk

to broadcast
**übertragen**
ew-behr-TRAH-gehn

magazine
**die Zeitschrift**
dee TSIET-shrihft

newspaper
**die Zeitung**
dee TSIE-toonk

radio
**das Radio**
dahs RAH-deeoh

television
**das Fernsehen**
dahs FEHRN-zeh-yehn

news broadcast
**die Nachrichtensendung**
dee NAHKH-reesh-tehn-zehn-doonk

weather forecast
**die Wettervorhersage**
dee VEH-tehr-fohr-hehr-zah-guh

| | | |
|---|---|---|
| blogosphere | **die Blogosphäre** | dee bloh-goh-SFEH-ruh |
| mass media | **die Massenmedien** | dee MAH-sehn-meh-deeuhn |
| news | **die Nachrichten** | dee NAKH-reesh-tehn |
| press | **die Presse** | dee PREH-suh |
| tabloid | **das Tabloid** | dahs TAH-bloh-eet |
| programme | **das Programm** | dahs proh-GRAHM |
| soap | **die Seifenoper** | dee ZIE-fehn-oh-pehr |
| drama | **das Drama** | dahs DRAH-mah |
| series | **die Serie** | dee ZEH-reeuh |
| film | **der Film** | dehr fihlm |
| documentary | **der Dokumentarfilm** | dehr doh-koo-mehn-TAHR-fihlm |
| music programme | **das Musikprogramm** | dahs moo-ZEEK-proh-grahm |
| sports programme | **das Sportprogramm** | dahs SHPOHRT-proh-grahm |
| talk show | **die Talkshow** | dee TOHK-show |
| episode | **die Folge** | dee FOHL-guh |
| business news | **die Wirtschaftsnachrichten** | dee VIHRT-shahfts-nahkh-reesh-tehn |
| sports report | **der Sportbericht** | dehr SHPOHRT-beh-reesht |
| book review | **die Buchrezension** | dee bookh-reh-tsehn-ZEEOHN |
| ad / advertisement | **die Werbung** | dee VEHR-boonk |

message
**die Nachricht**
dee NAHKH-reesht

address URL
**die Adresse URL**
dee ah-dreh-SUH oo-ehr-EHL

application / app
**die Applikation / die App**
dee ah-plee-kah-TSEEOHN / dee ehp

network
**das Netzwerk**
dahs NEHTS-vehrk

| | | |
|---|---|---|
| inbox | **der Posteingang** | dehr POHST-ien-gahnk |
| IP address | **die IP-Adresse** | dee ie-PEE-ah-dreh-suh |
| internet | **das Internet** | dahs IHN-tehr-neht |
| website | **die Webseite** | dee VEHB-zie-tuh |
| mail | **die Mail** | dee mehyl |
| search engine | **die Suchmaschine** | dee ZOOKH-mah-shee-nuh |
| to search | **suchen** | ZOO-khehn |
| to share | **teilen** | TIE-lehn |
| to log in | **sich einloggen** | zihsh IEN-loh-gehn |

to send
**senden**
zehn-dehn

login
**das Login**
dahs LOH-gihn

to log out
**sich ausloggen**
zihsh OWS-loh-gehn

| to upload | **hochladen** | HOHKH-lah-dehn |
| to download | **herunterladen** | heh-ROON-tehr-lah-dehn |
| to tag | **markieren** | mahr-KEE-rehn |
| to comment | **kommentieren** | koh-mehn-TEE-rehn |
| to publish | **veröffentlichen** | fehr-ER-fehnt-lee-shehn |
| to contact | **kontaktieren** | kohn-tahk-TEE-rehn |
| to receive | **bekommen** | beh-KOH-mehn |
| to add | **hinzufügen** | hihn-TSOO-few-gehn |

link
**der Link**
dehr lihnk

CD
**die CD**
dee tseh-DEH

CD-ROM
**die CD-ROM**
dee tseh-deh-ROHM

DVD
**die DVD**
dee deh-fow-DEH

mouse
**die Maus**
dee mows

keyboard
**die Tastatur**
dee tahs-tah-TOOR

USB flash drive
**der USB-Stick**
dehr oo-ehs-BEH-steek

laptop
**der Laptop**
dehr LEHP-tohp

modem
**der Modem**
dehr MOH-dehm

monitor
**der Monitor**
dehr MOH-nee-tohr

router
**der Router**
dehr ROO-tehr

tablet
**das Tablet**
dahs TEH-bleht

printer
**der Drucker**
dehr DROO-kehr

scanner
**der Scanner**
dehr SKEH-nehr

| | | | | | | |
|---|---|---|---|---|---|---|
| to copy | **kopieren** | koh-PEE-rehn | | to print | **drucken** | DROO-kehn |
| to delete | **löschen** | LER-shehn | | to save | **speichern** | SHPIE-shern |
| desktop | **der Desktop** | dehr DEHSK-tohp | | to scan | **scannen** | SKEH-nehn |
| file | **die Datei** | dee dah-TIE | | screenshot | **das Bildschirmfoto** | dahs BIHLT-shihrm-foh-toh |
| folder | **der Ordner** | dehr OHRD-nehr | | server | **der Server** | dehr SEHR-vehr |
| offline | **offline** | OHF-lien | | software | **die Software** | dee ZOHFT-vehr |
| online | **online** | OHN-lien | | to undo | **rückgängig machen** | REWK-gehn-gihk MAH-khehn |
| password | **das Passwort** | dahs PAHS-vohrt | | virus | **das Virus** | dahs VEE-roos |

at
**das At-Zeichen**
dahs EHT-tsie-shehn

hash
**das Rautenzeichen**
dahs ROW-tehn-tsie-shehn

percent
**das Prozent**
dahs proh-TSEHNT

circumflex
**das Zirkumflex**
dahs TSIHR-koom-flehx

ampersand
**das Et-Zeichen**
dahs EHT-tsie-shehn

asterisk
**das Sternchen**
dahs SHTEHRN-shehn

tilde
**die Tilde**
dee TIHL-duh

tab key
**die Tabulatortaste**
dee tah-boo-LAH-tohr-tahs-tuh

caps lock key
**die Feststelltaste**
dee FEHST-shtehl-tahs-tuh

shift key
**die Umschalttaste**
dee OOM-shahlt-tahs-tuh

ctrl (control) key
**die Befehlstaste**
dee beh-FEHLS-tahs-tuh

WIRELESS KEYBOARD K900

exclamation mark
**das Ausrufezeichen**
dahs OWS-roo-feh-tsie-shehn

alt (alternate) key
**die Alt (Alternate)-Taste**
dee AHLT (ahl-tehr-NEHYT)-tahs-tuh

spacebar key
**die Leertaste**
dee LEHR-tahs-tuh

minus / dash
**das Minus / der Bindestrich**
dahs MEE-noos /
dehr BIHN-deh-shtrihsh

plus
**das Plus**
dahs ploos

equal
**das Gleichheitszeichen**
dahs GLIESH-hiets-tsie-shehn

colon
**der Doppelpunkt**
dehr DOH-pehl-poonkt

semicolon
**das Semikolon**
dahs zeh-mee-KOH-lohn

dot / full stop
**der Punkt**
dehr poonkt

question mark
**das Fragezeichen**
dahs FRAH-geh-tsie-shehn

enter key
**die Entertaste**
dee EHN-tehr-tahs-tuh

forward slash
**der Schrägstrich**
dehr SHREHK-shtrihsh

back slash
**der Backslash**
dehr BEHK-slehsh

backspace key
**die Rücktaste**
dee REWK-tahs-tuh

delete (del) key
**die Löschtaste**
dee LERSH-tahs-tuh

amusement park
**der Freizeitpark**
dehr FRIE-tsieht-pahrk

aquarium
**das Aquarium**
dahs ah-KVAH-ree-oom

art gallery
**die Kunstgalerie**
dee KOONST-gah-leh-ree

art museum
**das Kunstmuseum**
dahs KOONST-moo-zeh-oom

botanical garden
**der Botanische Garten**
dehr boh-TAH-nih-shuh GAHR-tehn

cinema
**das Kino**
dahs KEE-noh

circus
**der Zirkus**
dehr TSIHR-koos

discotheque
**die Diskothek**
dee dihs-koh-TEHK

garden
**der Garten**
dehr GAHR-tehn

night club
**der Nachtklub**
dehr NAHKHT-kloop

exhibition
**die Ausstellung**
dee OWS-shteh-loonk

opera house
**das Opernhaus**
dahs OH-pehrn-hows

concert hall
**die Konzerthalle**
dee kohn-TSEHRT-hah-luh

park
**der Park**
dehr pahrk

planetarium
**das Planetarium**
dahs plah-neh-TAH-ree-oom

science museum
**das Wissenschaftsmuseum**
dahs VIH-sehn-shahfts-moo-zeh-oom

sights
**die Sehenswürdigkeiten**
dee ZEH-yehns-vewr-dihsh-kieh-tehn

theatre
**das Theater**
dahs teh-AH-tehr

tourist attraction
**die Touristenattraktion**
dee too-RIHST-tehn-ah-trahk-tseeohn

water park
**der Wasserpark**
dehr VAH-sehr-pahrk

zoo
**der Zoo**
dehr tsooh

accordion
**das Akkordeon**
dahs ah-KOHR-deh-ohn

bagpipes
**der Dudelsack**
dehr DOO-dehl-zahk

castanets
**die Kastagnetten**
dee kahs-tah-NYEH-tehn

cello
**das Cello**
dahs CHEH-loh

bugle
**das Horn**
dahs hohrn

banjo
**das Banjo**
dahs BAHN-goh

clarinet
**die Klarinette**
dee klah-ree-NEH-teh

cymbals
**die Becken**
dee BEH-kehn

drum
**die Trommel**
dee TROH-mehl

electric guitar
**elektrische Gitarre**
eh-LEHK-trih-shuh gee-TAH-ruh

flute
**die Flöte**
dee FLER-tuh

drum set
**das Schlagzeug**
dahs SHLAHK-tsoyk

harmonica
**die Mundharmonika**
dee MOONT-hahr-moh-nee-kah

guitar
**die Gitarre**
dee gee-TAH-ruh

grand piano
**der Konzertflügel**
dehr kohn-TSEHRT-flew-gehl

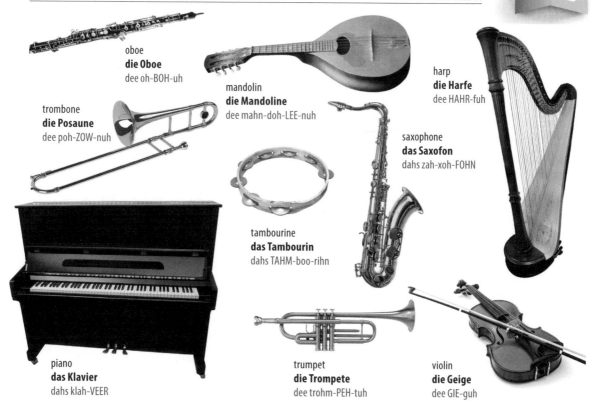

oboe
**die Oboe**
dee oh-BOH-uh

mandolin
**die Mandoline**
dee mahn-doh-LEE-nuh

harp
**die Harfe**
dee HAHR-fuh

trombone
**die Posaune**
dee poh-ZOW-nuh

saxophone
**das Saxofon**
dahs zah-xoh-FOHN

tambourine
**das Tambourin**
dahs TAHM-boo-rihn

piano
**das Klavier**
dahs klah-VEER

trumpet
**die Trompete**
dee trohm-PEH-tuh

violin
**die Geige**
dee GIE-guh

# Index